Nothing's wrong.

Also by David Kundtz

Stopping: How to Be Still When You Have to Keep Going
Quiet Mind: One-Minute Retreats from a Busy World

A Man's Guide
Nothing's
to managing
wrong.
his feelings

David Kundtz

CONARI PRESS

First published in 2004 by Conari Press,
an imprint of Red Wheel/Weiser, LLC
York Beach, ME
With offices at:
368 Congress Street
Boston, MA 02210
www.redwheelweiser.com

Some of the material in this book was self-published in 1990 and published by
Health Communications, Inc. under the title *Men and Feelings: Understanding the
Male Experience* in 1991.

Library of Congress Cataloging-in-Publication Data
Kundtz, David.
 Nothing's wrong : a man's guide to managing his feelings / David Kundtz.
   p. cm.
Includes bibliographical references and index.
 ISBN 1-57324-915-7
 1. Men—Psychology. 2. Emotions. I. Title.
 BF692.5.K86 2004
 155.6'32—dc22
                          2003017458
Typeset in Bulmer MT
Printed in Canada
TCP
11 10 09 08 07 06 05 04
 8 7 6 5 4 3 2 1

For
Louise - Ewald - Andy
with love and gratitude

contents

acknowledgments

This book is the culmination of a long-term project that means a great deal to me. It began with a single page of notes for a client. Indeed, it has been from my practice of family counseling that I have had opportunities to learn firsthand from clients—men and women—about the topic of men and feelings.

Thus I must first thank the wonderful clients of my practice for trusting me with the stories of their lives. They are a deep blessing to me.

I also want to thank Mary Jane Ryan, whose skillful editing always makes me look better than I deserve, and Brendan Collins, Ph.D., and Randy Marcotte for reading the text and suggesting helpful changes. Special thanks to Jan Johnson, publisher at Conari Press, for wisdom, patience, and for believing in the work, and to all the great people at Red Wheel/Weiser/Conari Press.

In addition, I appreciate the support of: Doug Jennette, MSW, a therapist in Raleigh, North Carolina, for long-term interest and a helpful critique; John Buchanan of the Center for Character-Based Leadership in Minneapolis, for his support, encouragement, and help in the preparation of the text;

Bob Stenberg for continuing support and suggestions for the text; Ewald Kundtz, for textual suggestions and assistance in the business end of writing; Allen Klein, Alice Potter, Amy Berger, and Ann Mahoney, fellow writers, for their ideas and care. Thank you all!

The young man who has not wept is a savage,
and the old man who will not laugh is a fool.

—GEORGE SANTAYANA 1863–1952

SPANISH-AMERICAN PHILOSOPHER

When it comes to shaping our decisions and our actions, feeling counts every bit as much—and often more—than thought.

—DANIEL GOLEMAN

AMERICAN PSYCHOLOGIST

author's note

In all the case histories and examples of this book, especially those from my practice as a family therapist, all the names and other nonessential facts have been deliberately scrambled and changed in order to protect rights of confidentiality and privacy.

Saving Half Your Life

You are reading the first words of the first sentence of the book that could save your life. Well, half your life.

This Book Is for Men

Too many guys of all ages do not have about half the information we need in order to achieve success in life. The part that we actually get is the thinking half. That's the part that deals with facts, figures, and procedures. For the most part, we men do well when we're dealing with this kind of factual information—really well.

The part we don't get is the emotional half. How do all the things that happen to us make us feel? You could say that we lost this half before we ever got it. Something in us—something urgently important—never gets life at all. It remains asleep, as good as dead. There are reasons for this—we'll name a few later on—but whatever the reasons, the smart, successful guys will get this information. And the sooner you get it, the easier your life.

Don't get the wrong idea. This is not touchy-feely stuff. Many of us don't much like that. This is about learning a skill and developing a process that most of us never got a chance to practice. I have no power to tell you what to feel nor any interest in doing so; my purpose is rather to help you identify and express *whatever* you feel in a healthy way and to be comfortable with the feelings of others.

Nothing's Wrong is intended simply to serve as a guide for men to understand how to deal with their feelings.

Women are warmly welcomed, but this book is written for males, from teenagers to grandfathers. The basic ideas presented here apply to everyone, but they are specifically designed for guys who never got a map for navigating the highways and byways of the emotional realm.

"What's wrong?"

I may not be totally perfect, but parts of me are excellent.

—ASHLEIGH BRILLIANT,
AMERICAN ARTIST AND WRITER

How many times we have heard the question "What's wrong?" It generally comes when we are noticeably feeling something. Our response to the question invariably is "Nothing's wrong," which always seems to be the wrong answer, at least not the answer that was expected or desired. The questioner is often—but not always—a woman.

Our answer of "Nothing's wrong" is actually a true answer. In other words, there's nothing wrong with us. That's true.

However, time and again we are unable to get to the next part; we get stuck with "Nothing's wrong." After we say what we know in our gut to be true—there's nothing wrong with us— too often we stand there puzzled and unable to proceed. What comes next is only our unspoken question: *Now what?*

Nothing's wrong with us. We are not deficient in some essential way, faulty from birth, somehow damaged goods, even though we are often perceived that way. Our problem comes not from some essential flaw but from the failure—our own as well as others'—to recognize our particular way of expressing and managing feelings, and from our lack of training and encouragement to do this in a way that is natural for us.

The lack of recognition and encouragement of a man's way of dealing with emotions is deeply ingrained in our cultural assumptions, so much so that the "unfeeling male" is a stereotype, a cultural joke, often accepted by both men and women.

The title of this book, *Nothing's Wrong,* is intended to say that there is nothing at all wrong with the way men express and manage feelings if—and it's a big if—they are given the chance to know and affirm the way that is natural to them, the way nature has equipped them to do it, which, as we will see, is often not the way women express and manage their feelings.

Guts

I mentioned that we know the truth of the title in our guts. I believe that *guts* is a good word for the way men do emotions. While women often "feel from the heart," we "feel from the gut." For many of us the source of our feelings seems to be, more than anywhere else, in the pit of our stomachs. It is often the place where we carry our tension and feel the effects of stress. When we give an emotional response to some event or situation, it is often a "gut response," something from a source that is deep, visceral, urgent, and primal.

I like the word also because it takes courage—or guts—to tackle the subject of this book. It takes a twenty-first-century kind of courage. The frontier we are exploring here is not an uncharted coast or interstellar space. We are exploring a personal and social process of the contemporary male. Our challenging frontiers are very different from our forebears', but the territory often feels the same: unknown and foreign.

The focus here is clear and specific: how men can become skilled and confident with the feeling part of life. Think of it as the course no one ever offered you: Feelings 101. I have tried to keep the journey short and sweet, the work light, and the payoff huge.

Welcome.

one

Strangers No More

Let's begin with two guys: the man *on* the moon and the man *in* the moon.

We know who the man *on* the moon is. He's the astronaut walking on the lunar surface, brought there by logic, nerve, and courage. He's the "thinking guy" of calculations and logic, predictable and exact. He is the man who is very interested in the external things of the world, like space travel and geology (as well as stocks and bonds, planes and boats, baseball and rugby, cell phones and fast cars). He has steely nerves and determination; he's actually walked on the moon and returned to earth to tell about it.

Everyone admires him.

We also know who the man *in* the moon is—or do we? He's not so easy to know. He's a trickster. He has a vivid imagination and dreams a lot. He's full of surprises. He has a sly grin on his face, and we're not sure just what he's up to. He's the "feeling guy" of deep emotions, soulful humor, and wild zaniness (as well as art and beauty, jokes and parties, tears and smiles, rough games and laughter). He is spontaneous and unpredictable. He's the man who is interested in the deep inner life of possibilities and potential miracles. He's full of life and play and understanding.

Everyone loves him.

Nothing's Wrong is based on the idea that we need to be *both* these guys: the gutsy, thinking astronaut *and* the gutsy, fun-loving man in the moon. Because to be one without being the other is to be only half a person, to live only half a life.

There are several ways to talk about this half-life. You could say many men have a well developed thinking part and an under-developed feeling part. Or males are more logical and less sen-sitive; we are more serious, less playful. We are better at being workers than at being friends.

Women might say about us: *He never wants to talk very much* or *I never know what he's really feeling* or *He can be kind, but he doesn't let you in* or *I never seem to get to know him.*

Many of us males are playing the game of life with half the team missing. And we often wonder what's going on, why things don't work out better for us.

Men, Moon, and Mountain

Here are a couple of stories about these two guys, astronaut-thinking guy and man-in-the-moon-feeling guy.

The first one happened in 1972—on the moon. Did you ever see the video of *Apollo 16* astronaut John Young as he jumped up and down and waved his arms wildly during his walk on the moon? His behavior had nothing to do with the scientific purpose of the expedition. He was just having fun. He looked like an excited kid on a trampoline. The guys at Mission Control in Houston were probably not impressed. *What the hell is Young doing? He's not supposed to do that!* His kids watching on TV probably got a hoot out of it. *Wow! Look at Dad!*

In those few seconds, Young became a great example of both parts of male life: thinking (technical/logical) and feeling (artistic/spontaneous). He was, in that happy moment, the man on the moon *and* the man in the moon.

Here's another story. It also takes place up in the air, on the top of Mount Everest, the highest mountain in the world, located in the rugged and remote northern highlands of Tibet. In 1953 Edmund Hillary, an explorer from New Zealand who was leading a British expedition, successfully scaled Mount Everest. He was the first human being to achieve this incredible feat.

When Hillary completed his historic act of reaching the summit, exhausted but happy, the first thing he did was thrust the British flag deep into the snow to proclaim that he had conquered the mountain.

But he wasn't the only one there. His companion and guide, Tenzing Norgay, had also made the historic climb. Norgay was a Sherpa, one of the legendary mountain guides from northern Tibet. He was raised in a simple rural family, with a very different background from Edmund Hillary.

As you might expect, Tenzing Norgay expressed himself in a different way. Upon arriving at the summit of the great mountain, he knelt down in the snow and prayed to the gods of the mountain, asking their forgiveness for disturbing their peace.

One man proclaimed his conquering achievement. The other prayed to the gods for pardon. The point I want to make is this: *We need both. Because we are both.* One is not right while the other is wrong. One is not weird and the other normal. No. *They are both healthy expressions of the male life.*

In this instance, you could say that Hillary expressed the thinking part and Norgay expressed the feeling part. But we know from their lives and writings that Norgay understood and applauded Hillary's flag-thrust, while Hillary respected and affirmed Norgay's prayer.

The one needs the other. Even more, in order to live a complete life, each needs to *become* the other. I want to make clear from the beginning that I do *not* label one as good and the other as bad. That is the last thing I want to do. Both of these male aspects are good, and we must welcome both of them into our lives.

Miseducation

One's happiness depends less on what he knows than on what he feels.

—Liberty Hyde Bailey (1858–1954),

botanist and horticulturist

As males, our biggest problem is that on the subject of emotions, our culture is deeply biased. There are reasons why most boys and men, probably including you, have been "emotionally miseducated," a term I've borrowed from Michael Thompson and Dan Kindlon's book *Raising Cain.* What they mean is that the combined forces of society steer a young male "away from his inner world." This has an effect, they say, "even on the youngest boy, who learns quickly . . . that he must hide his feelings and silence his fears." We carry that attitude, alive and well, into our adult lives.

I believe this is true for all men: young and old, highly educated and less educated, raised in well-to-do families or in poor families, extroverts and introverts, straight and gay, urban businessmen and country ranchers, steel workers and family therapists, managers and employees, basketball players and poets—*all* of us.

While society tolerates some of what it sees as "male emotions," like anger and aggression, it is generally uncomfortable with the free expression of all feelings by boys and men, and strongly resists teaching and promoting them. So our culture tries actively to steer you in the wrong direction. That's something to take note of. As a result, of course, most men are good at thinking and not so good at feeling.

But that's not all. There is also a physical basis for the way we are with our feelings. It's the way our brains are "wired." I'll refer to a few of these characteristics later.

Putting Words on Feelings

Given the culture in which we've been raised, it's no wonder that many of us are challenged by the feeling part of life. We often can't seem to recognize and talk about the feelings we are having at any given moment.

What we do instead is run away or cover up. As soon as we feel something, or someone else in our presence is feeling something—especially if it's a strong feeling like fear or attraction—we run from it before it has a chance to let us know it's there, much less get expressed. Running means changing the subject, distracting yourself with some other activity, or moving on to something new.

Or we cover it. With TV, music, sports, humor, sex, laughter. Anything that covers over and hides the feelings that are there.

So when someone asks us what we're feeling, we can often truthfully say, "Oh, nothing." We're not lying, because we run so quickly from the feeling or cover it so well that we literally don't know it is there.

Here are stories that two men, Jim and Derek, tell about themselves when they were boys. I want to start there because that's when it starts.

■ Jim's Story ■

Jim is forty-two, a civil engineer, husband, and father of two: "When I was a junior in high school I was fairly popular. In fact, everyone was expecting me to be elected homecoming king. But when the votes were in, I lost. I was fourth out of five. Everyone was surprised, including me. But what I said was 'Oh, it's OK, I didn't really expect to get it. It's no problem. It's nothing.' These were my typical responses to my parents, teachers, and friends.

"But what I was really feeling was painful embarrassment and shame. In fact, I can still feel it now as I talk about it, after all these years! Now, of course, I know what I was feeling, but for too long I just didn't allow most of my feelings to come out."

Any normal human being would have those feelings. But Jim ran from them. Changed the topic. Got involved in something else. Denied any negative feelings. Probably put on his headphones and blasted the music. "This was exactly the occasion," he adds, "when I started a pattern of nonfeeling."

There's a name for the condition I'm talking about: *Alexithymia*. It's from Greek words meaning "no words for feelings." A few of us guys have it really bad; most of us have at least a light case of it.

The bad news is that it does a lot of damage to us. The good news is that, in the vast majority of cases, it's fixable.

Alexithymia:

"Difficulty in describing or recognizing one's emotions . . ." The word is "used to describe persons who define emotions only in terms of bodily sensations or behavioral reaction . . ."

Psychiatric Dictionary

> "A mood in which one has a constricted emotional life, diminished ability to fantasize, and a virtual inability to articulate emotions."
>
> *Essential Psychopathology*
>
> "People with alexithymia lack words for their feelings. Indeed, they seem to lack feelings altogether, although this may actually be because of their inability to *express* emotion rather than an absence of emotion."
>
> Daniel Goleman, *Emotional Intelligence*

■ Derek's Story: "I Won't Tell You" ■

For most of us, these patterns began when we were boys. The story of Derek, now forty-four, begins during the end of his senior year in high school. This was a kid who had been in trouble forever. He was a middle child in a large and gregarious family. At this late date in the school year, it was doubtful if he would make the grades to graduate.

Then he got caught by the vice principal smoking pot in the school parking lot. That was the point at which Derek literally shut up. He wouldn't talk to anyone—family, friends, school counselor, pastor, teachers, or police—no one. He'd just look at the ground and shake his head.

His story slowly moves forward with very little life. He had to do community service for using a controlled substance. He did not graduate from high school. He got an unchallenging job and just sort of existed. Only now, in midlife, is he coming to his full emotional life.

By titling Derek's story "I *won't* tell you," I make an assumption that he could have told us if he wanted. While I think that's true, I don't really know. That's the frustrating thing about Derek and so many like him. We just don't know what's going on in their inner life. They won't or can't tell us. He had no words for his feelings, which remained locked up deep inside him.

■ Steve's Story: "I Can't Tell You" ■

Here's a story of a man who is very good at the thinking side. He is a member of Mensa—only very high IQs invited. His name is Steve. He and his wife, Amy, are in their late thirties, with two young kids, their own home, and successful working lives. They have come to see me, a family therapist, because their marriage is troubled.

During our fifth or sixth session, without warning, Amy says she believes their marriage cannot survive and she wants a divorce. Bam! just like that.

To this sobering announcement Steve reacts with a sad, vacant stare into space. It lasts a long fifteen seconds; no one says a word. I am as surprised as he is. Then, without saying anything, he calmly stands up, picks up his coat and briefcase, and walks out of my office.

Jump ahead two weeks.

After several attempts, I convince Steve to come in on his own "to talk about it." When he comes to my office, I can feel him bristle. He doesn't want to be here. We start talking; or rather, I start talking. From him I get nothing but grunts, noises, or shakes of the head. Clearly he is in pain. A couple times he glances at me, silently begging me to end the torture and let him go. He just can't say much of anything.

After one particularly long period of silence, I notice I am really getting annoyed and think to myself, *This must be what his wife feels.* Then I ask, "Well, Steve, what about just telling me, briefly, what you are feeling right now, knowing that your wife intends to divorce you?"

His response begins slowly, then quickly builds force as his eyes snap wide to attention, rise up and rivet me. His face becomes flushed, his body rigid, his fists clenched, and his look enraged.

Then he bolts from his seat, storms across the room, turns back toward me—now fevered and furious—raises his arms high (to attack? to entreat?) and literally screams, "You sound just like my wife! Don't you see?" And then even louder and more anguished, "I don't know what I'm feeling!"

When my heart returns to its normal beat and I take a deep breath or two—he is now slumped in his chair, spent and embarrassed—I say in a quiet voice, "Oh."

After a moment I said it again, "Oh." I could only hope the simple word expressed what I wanted him to know: that I heard him, not just his words—I'm sure half the building heard those—but him.

More importantly, I wanted him to know that I actually believed him: he did not know what he was feeling about his marriage, his possible divorce, and even about his wife.

Steve simply did not know his emotional state, and thus could not put it into words. He knew he was in pain, but beyond that, he simply didn't know. It wasn't that he didn't want to know. In fact he did want to know. It wasn't that he really knew but just wouldn't tell me. No, he really *didn't know.* He truly had no words for his feelings.

Steve was a man in his late thirties when this happened. He was so used to not knowing his feelings that he didn't know that he didn't know.

It's Not Too Late

In this situation—not being able to put into words the emotions you are experiencing—many men find we are misjudged as stuck-up or stubborn or even stupid. Sometimes we even judge ourselves with those words. But in the vast majority of situations this is not true. Almost always what we are going through are the effects of our lack of training in the ways of dealing with feelings.

Many times, when the feelings finally do come out, they come out in an explosion, like Steve's did. And often they get us into trouble. At best we're accused of overreacting; at worst we're seen as fearsome or violent. It's a no-win situation.

There's a point I want to make with the stories of Jim, Derek, and Steve: If you begin *now* to find ways to attach words—or some other healthy means of expression—to your feelings, you can avoid the sad situations that the three of them got into. This is indeed what you are doing by reading this book. It's never too late!

Today Steve continues his slow but sure journey to emotional fitness. Although he and his wife separated for a few months, they both did four months of counseling and he joined a weekly men's group. They got together again and are now giving the marriage a second chance. In fact, it is from our work together several years ago that this book began to take shape.

And Derek? It's an on-going story. When we last met, the signs were good. The reason for these changes is that he had "met someone" and was very interested in her. But she did not want a half-living partner. I'm betting he's been successful. He was really tired of living half a life.

Emotional Literacy

In our culture, feelings are not talked about very much. Unfortunately, you can't take a course in feelings at any school. All human beings, male and female, have feelings and have the capacity for the full range of emotional expression. But sometimes boys and men act, and are treated, as if we just don't *have* any feelings.

Another way to talk about this is with the term "emotional literacy," which is about being comfortable with the language of feelings. We all have a history—the stories of our successes and failures—of dealing with our feelings, and it is helpful to know what your history is.

Your Relationship to Feelings

Here are a few questions, broadly based on Claude Steiner's *When a Man Loves a Woman,* to help you find out about your relationship with feelings. Read them over and keep track of your "yeses" and "noes."

1. Do your feelings sometimes puzzle you? Are you sometimes unable to understand them or know what to do about them? *Yes*

2. Do your feelings sometimes get out of control? Like a feeling of anger? Or feeling sad and depressed? *Yes*

3. Do you sometimes feel very alone and left out, with the sense that you are missing out on something important? *Yes*

4. Do people complain that you are a loner? Different from everyone else? That you are cold? Stuck-up? Mean? *Yes*

5. Do you have trouble getting to know friends more than just casually? *Yes*

6. Do you experience your feelings of liking others as coming and going and changing quickly? *No*

7. Are you embarrassed to ask for what you want or to talk about being hurt? *Yes*

8. Do you have trouble crying? Or do you cry a lot? *No / No*

9. Do you avoid emotional situations like good-byes? Or people who are grieving or sick? *No / No*

10. Are you embarrassed when someone shows affection for you in public? *No*

11. Do you sometimes avoid feelings by expecting the females in your life—family member, wife, friend—to live your emotional life for you? *Yes*

If you answered "yes" to some or all of these questions or if your "noes" were weak or doubtful, then you're just like most of us guys. Like the rest of us, you have a degree of *emotional illiteracy;* you are sometimes at a loss when it comes to knowing what to do about feelings. "Now what do I do?" is often as far as we get.

The Inner Life

> When I do good, I feel good. When I do bad,
> I feel bad. And that's my religion.
>
> —ABRAHAM LINCOLN

For many, "the inner life" might not be a very hot topic. The sound of it might even make you nervous. This is where "guts" comes into the process. Right now is when I need you to hang in there. Why? Because lifelong misery begins right here. The very words *inner life* can make us nervous. It is precisely here, your inner life, where most guys get into trouble and stay there for their whole lives. Bear with me for a few paragraphs and I think you'll see it.

First, what do I mean by the "inner life"? There are a lot of ways to answer that. You actually know what it is, of course, but it is difficult to describe. So that we're on the same page, here is a free-flowing description of some of the things that make up the inner life.

The inner life is the life you live when you are alone and just thinking. Everything that you fantasize and imagine is part of it. It is what you feel when you see someone you like, or dislike. It's what you experience when you think of an enjoyable event or a terrible one. It's everything in your life that is not visible in some way—love, understanding, jealousy, and those kinds of intangible values. It's what moves you, what motivates you to do what you do and be who you are. Your inner life determines your character, your qualities, your vices, your virtues, what you value a lot, what you don't value at all. It's your loves, your hates, your fun, your fears—but especially it's your secrets.

It's the part you can keep hidden, but it's the part that everyone sees the results of. That's because your inner life determines your response to your "outer life" or the part of your life that others can perceive, like what you say, where you go, your gestures, your words, your smiles, your scowls. In other words, the inner life has its hands on the controls of your being and tells the outer life what to do and what not to do, how to respond, what to avoid. Your inner life is *everything you feel,* the entire range of your emotions, and therefore ultimately controls your life, whether you are aware of it or not.

Keep three things in mind about the inner life:

1. There is a man's way to navigate the inner life (The Three Steps to Emotional Fitness in chapter 4)

2. The more congruence (or agreement, or harmony) between your inner life and your outer life, the more integrated or mature your personality.

3. The inner life has the power.

Some of the other words that many of us use when talking about the inner life are: soul, mind, self, and spirit.

Religion is very interested in the inner life. In fact, religion is the primary practice that some men use to navigate the territory. Everything presented in this book is totally compatible with the practice of any and all religious faith. It is equally compatible with a life that holds no religious practice at all, or, like Abraham Lincoln (quoted above), with a life that follows its own kind of religion.

At this point maybe you're thinking something like: *Wait a minute! Wait a minute! Alexithymia? Emotionally illiterate? No inner life?* To paraphrase a gang member in *West Side Story*, "Gee, Officer Krupke, no wonder I'm a mess!"

But wait, please! These are all really the same thing: limited skill with feelings. They're just different ways of looking at it. So no, you're not a mess. You carry on just fine. Many of us have amazing skills at "faking it" and getting through life quite well without half of our resources.

On the other hand, yes, part of you, like most of us guys, probably is a bit of a mess. My guess is that a few of us are in pretty rough shape in this regard, another few of us are real emotional pros, and most of us are on the high or low end of muddling through.

It takes some guts to admit that. I hope you see that while it certainly takes guts to follow the astronaut to the moon, which is exploring the outer life, it takes equally as much courage—or more—to follow the man in the moon on the journey within. The path you are now walking is a path of courage.

The bottom line? If your inner life is taken care of, it will respond just as your body does to good care. It will not only survive, it will thrive. By becoming skillful in the area of your feelings, you are caring for your inner life. You're taking care of the real you, looking out for Number One, not in the way of selfishness, but in the way of responsibility, which is another name for maturity.

A Question

A person buying products in a supermarket is
in touch with his deepest emotions.

—JOHN KENNETH GALBRAITH, ECONOMIST

The question that chapter 1 leads to is this: Are you aware of your feelings and can you express them successfully? This is a question that only you can answer. Spend some time thinking about it and see what you come up with. Here's the question again: *Are you aware of your feelings and can you express them successfully?*

Very few, if any, of us would respond with a definitive yes or no to that question. Some of us might have a more or less clear answer. But you are not unusual if you do not have sufficient awareness of your feelings to make an informed answer right away. Many of us are not at all sure what degree of skill we have with feelings. Or again, you may feel embarrassed or uncomfortable with the question itself. Or you may be puzzled by the question, still not sure just what I'm asking.

If you answered "no" or "I'm not sure," or even if you answered "yes" or "I think so," the information in this book can help you determine if your answer is accurate or help you clarify your doubts.

One thing is sure: when you finish this brief but adventurous journey, chances are excellent that you'll be better able to get more of what you want in life. Why? Because you'll be leading a *whole* life. The astronaut/thinking you will shake hands with the man in the moon/feeling you and they will be strangers no more; they'll be friends and allies, united in the one you.

A Few Suggestions for Review

- Which of the two are you most like, the logical astronaut *70%* walking on the moon or the unpredictable, playful man in the moon? *30%*
- Of course either answer to that question is correct because both are good and necessary. Maybe you have parts of both. If so, can you put an approximate percentage on each?
- Jim, Derek, and Steve were all unable to "speak" in some way. They couldn't get what was happening in their inner lives into the outer world. Thus they could not accomplish what they needed and wanted. You ever been there?

two

Feelings Just Are

Just What Is a Feeling, *Exactly?*

That was a question a client asked me, with an emphasis on the "exactly." It's a great question because it is so direct, to the point, and so difficult to answer exactly and correctly.

But because it is so important, and because I didn't have a ready-made answer, he and I spent a lot of time trying to get the right words. Here's what my client came up with: *Your gut response to anything at any moment of your life.* I like that answer. I think it's an especially good answer for men.

> A feeling is your gut response to anything at any moment of your life.

Here are some other possible answers:

- Feelings are your automatic reactions to life or to any of its many aspects.
- Feelings are your instinctive responses to the persons, things, and events of the world—the small world you live in and the big world all around you.

- Feelings are urges to act, or movements from within you toward some action, which include thoughts as well as psychological and biological states.

But here's the answer I like best: *Feelings are the internal responses that are going on in you as you are going through life.* I like the word *responses* here because it implies a readiness to give forth. These responses are to the realities inside you and to all that comes at you from the outside world. They are the *most powerful of all influences on the quality of your entire life.* That means—I'll risk saying it again—if you are good at the feeling part of life, your chances of success and happiness are hugely increased. I mean enormously.

> **Feelings are the internal attitudes and responses that are going on in you as you are going through life.**

This definition emphasizes that feelings begin their lives internally. They are in you; they are a part of you; you generate them. Even if they are a response to what is happening outside of you, they come from within. Two people can experience the same event at the same time and have widely different feelings in response.

Sometimes the words *emotion* or *affect* are used instead of *feeling,* and they can often mean the same thing. Psychiatrist Willard Gaylin, in his book *Feelings: Our Vital Signs,* makes these distinctions: *Emotion* is the general term that includes feeling, biological states, and even chemical changes. *Affect* refers to one's overall emotional tone as others perceive it. *Feeling* is the subjective awareness of one's own emotional state.

I like the word *feeling* because it's simpler and more personal, and it gets closer to the area where we have trouble, our personal awareness. Thus, it's also more challenging for men. For example, when you hear or say the word *feelings* do you experience some discomfort? Does it sound "soft" or "feminine" or "unmanly" or otherwise suspect? Bingo! That's paydirt. And that's part of our challenge.

Why Are Feelings Important?

Feelings are everywhere—be gentle.

—J. MASAI, PHYSICIST

How can I tell you about the importance of feelings? It's like trying to tell you of the importance of the floorboards in your home. Most of the time we never really think about floorboards, but what if your home had none? There would be nothing to stand on. The same with feelings. You rarely think about them, but like the floorboards that support you, they are your grounding, the base on which your whole life stands.

All life involves feelings, all the time. They rarely stop. The more significant a moment of life, the more intensely feelings are involved. The way you handle your feelings can allow you to soar to the stars or get stuck in the mud.

Feeling is everything. Well, almost everything. Feelings are your guide to goodness and fun, your warning of pain and danger. The whole day long they are "talking" to you: *This is fantastic! That sucks! Look at me! Get outta here quick! Watch out!*

Following Karl

Try to think back to when you were fifteen. (For some of you it's a long time, for others it may be recent, or even current, history.) Let's follow Karl for the first hour of a day in his life. He's a fifteen-year-old high school sophomore:

(Alarm rings.) *Oh no, I don't wanna get up yet! I was dreaming of that great . . .* (Mother's voice: "Karl, get up! You'll be late!") *Oh shit! I'm gonna be late again!* (Jumps out of bed and into the bathroom.) *God, I've got that damn math test today and I'm gonna totally blow it . . . another D and no allowance increase . . .* (Gets dressed, looks in the mirror.) *I hate what I look like; no wonder Jennifer doesn't even look at me!* (Father's voice at breakfast: "You're not going to school wearing that, are you? Do they allow that?") *My parents must hate me. Why did they even have me? I'm getting outta here.* (Leaves breakfast, gets coat and books, leaves house. Parents look at each other and roll their eyes.)

Maybe all his days don't begin like this, but this one did.

And this is just the beginning. Already in the first hour of the day Karl has experienced many feelings: *dreamy, warm,* and *comfortable; panicky* and *worried; concerned* for grades and money; *discouraged* at his appearance; *frustrated* with his par-

ents; and probably a whole lot more. And truth be told, probably the *first* feeling he was aware of upon awakening was *horny*.

Karl at fifteen is oblivious to how to deal with or respond to
all that he's feeling. He's just zooming ahead. That's a disadvantage, to be sure. But we can cut him some slack because he's
a kid. However, Karl at thirty-two and still not sure what to do
with his feeling life—this is more than a simple disadvantage.
It's tragic.

Feelings put you in contact with life so that you know that
this is *your* life you're living and not someone else's idea—your
father's maybe?—of what your life should be.

Have you ever heard that someone in a life-threatening
situation said, "My entire life flashed before my eyes!"? Well,
wouldn't it be a disaster if someone else's life flashed before
your eyes! It's *your* life you must lead, and your feelings are
the key to ensuring that happens.

> "Not to be aware of one's feelings, not to understand
> them or know how to use or express them, is worse
> than being blind, deaf or paralyzed. Not to feel is not
> to be alive."
>
> Dr. David Viscott

Not being aware of your feelings can make you ill, both
physically and mentally. Too many men are either sick or in
some kind of trouble because of their failure to cope in a healthy
way with feelings.

We may think that guys who get into trouble with the law, with violence, with alcohol or drug use, are simply bad. I believe in many cases they have a lot of feelings that they don't know what to do with, so they do the wrong thing; not because they're basically bad, but because they just don't know what else to do with all that energy. It's got to go somewhere.

■ George's Story ■

George was fifty-two when he came for his first counseling session. He was nervous and reluctant. Being in my office felt like a defeat to him. He was an impressive guy: successful, good-looking, well educated, and articulate. Why did he come to counseling? "I'm single and I don't want to be."

He told a long and painful history of one romantic relationship after another in which the woman he was seeing dropped him. Recently he became involved in searching for a wife in a foreign country through the Internet. That didn't work out either. He was in a lot of pain, which was hard for him to acknowledge. And he was frustrated.

It soon became clear that George blamed the women he was involved with for the failure of their relationships. It was all their fault. He could not acknowledge that there was something in him that was keeping him from a successful relationship. When I approached that possibility, he would simply list all his positive characteristics: understanding, kindness, generosity, good listening skills, thoughtfulness, and so on. These were, no doubt, true.

He was at a genuine dead end. He felt that he had literally bent over backward and tried everything to make his relationships work. And they never did. It made him mad as hell, but he couldn't say that directly. I only noticed it in the way he held his body, the way he spoke with a fixed smile and careful words, and in the deep underlay of anger that energized everything he did—but only indirectly.

I decided on an end-run approach rather than a direct hit in the middle of the line. "Tell me the story of your life," I said. His response was immediate and clear. He said things like "that has nothing to do with why I'm here" and "it's not at all interesting or significant." He did not want to tell me the story of his life. He wanted help with this particular problem and he wanted it now. Can I provide that or should he go to someone else? He said all of this in a very polite and controlled way.

"But I need to know you a bit," I said. "I can't try to find out what's going on if I don't know something about you and your life up to this point. I'm sure you see that we can't do anything with the women who have been part of your life, so we have to begin with you."

So, very reluctantly, he told me the story of his fifty-two years in about a minute and a half. But it was a beginning.

Do you see what's going on with George? His inner life was in complete lockup. Women would no doubt see that this man was not able to be intimate—emotionally close and available— and they lost interest, no matter how attractive his other characteristics. They simply would never "get in" to his real self.

George had a breakthrough. It happened when he finally was able to get really mad at me for pushing him. His expression of anger opened the way for all the other pent-up emotional cargo to come rolling out as well. It came like a torrent, and it changed his life.

Much later, when he was reflecting on the way he used to be, he said: "I just didn't know!" If he said it once, he said it a million times, shaking his head, "I just didn't know!" "What, George? What didn't you know?" I asked him. "I didn't know what was going on in me. I was really afraid to look. I was just a big mess of stuff!" "A big mess of stuff" is his— uncharacteristic—phrase.

The "big mess of stuff" that George didn't understand was a combination of many different feelings that were all bunched up together inside him. He didn't have the skill to identify and deal with them in a way that could have helped him be emotionally available rather than locked up and isolated.

George made it. He's lost the controlling affect, and now he'll tell you about himself. And, yes, he's married and a father. But there still are way too many "Georges" out there who don't make it. They cause a great deal of harm to themselves and to all of us.

The Kinds of Feelings

There are many kinds of feelings. They can be positive or negative. That is, they can be fun or they can plunge you deeply into the no-fun zone. They can make you feel great and ready for anything or make you feel totally miserable.

Most feelings have both mental and physical manifestations. When you face a fearful situation, you might be conjuring up visions of terror and bloody disaster in your mind, while your body is doing its part as your stomach turns somersaults. Sexual feelings almost always have both physical and mental manifestations.

Feelings can be conscious or unconscious. Even the ones we are unaware of can influence how we feel at any moment.

The Middle Range

Feelings can be weak or strong. That is, they can practically knock you off your feet or barely touch you at all. At one time, say if someone important to you is very sick or dies, your whole life could be overwhelmed with feelings of loss and grief. Another time, you might barely sense a feeling of irritation, when a neighbor, for example, plays the TV too loud.

Mostly, however, our feelings fall somewhere in the middle range of emotional intensity, with only minor ups and downs in our emotional roller coaster. I believe this is very important to understand, especially for men.

For most human beings, extremely strong emotions are, if not rare, certainly less common. If you've ever participated in sports or watched a game on TV, you have no doubt about men's ability to express strong emotions, both positive and negative. They are right out there for all to see. This has led some sociologists to conclude that one of the main reasons men love sports, both as spectators and participants, is that it's the only time they really feel alive. One might say, more analytically, that it is the only time some men really feel anything strongly.

Likewise, we have little trouble with the low-intensity emotions—we get along just fine dealing with the little annoyances and little joys of life.

The middle range is where we get into trouble. These are not the many feelings that often go unnoticed because of their brevity; nor are they the occasional really big ones that get full expression. These are the angers, joys, frustrations, guilts, excitements, and sadnesses that happen all the time, day-in and day-out, and are the most influential of all our feelings, especially in our relationships with other people. Here, in the middle range, is where we falter. I think it is because we become self-conscious. The little ones don't cause any ruckus, the big ones take on a life of their own. The ones in the middle range we have to deal with.

Researchers argue over which emotions are primary, the ones from which all others come. Here are some candidates for the list, along with some of their relatives:

Anger: rage, resentment, hatred, violence

Grief: sorrow, gloom, loneliness, depression, sadness

Fear: anxiety, dread, fright, terror

Pleasure: happiness, joy, relief, bliss, sensuality, ecstasy

Love: friendliness, trust, kindness, infatuation

Wonder: shock, astonishment, amazement, surprise

Contempt: disdain, scorn, revulsion, aversion

Shame: guilt, embarrassment, dishonor, regret, contrition

The number and variety of feelings are endless. Look at the List of Feelings on pages 36–37. These are just a few of a limitless number. The list is meant to help you get into the habit of recognizing feelings and of realizing their endless variety. Read it over and see which ones you've known. From now on, you can refer to this list when you're feeling something, but can't quite figure out what you're feeling.

"Feelings Stew"

There's something about feelings that we have to get clear at this point. It's this: Feelings are not always logical or orderly; in fact most of the time they are illogical and disorderly.

Recall George's keen description of himself: "A big mess of stuff." That jumble of emotions—let's call it "Feelings Stew"—is most typical when we are adolescents, but it never really goes away. You can feel two opposing feelings at the very same time, and sometimes there are more than just two. Love and hate, suspicion and trust, joy and sorrow, sadness and happiness, all in the same person, all at the same moment. It happens all the time. It's conflicting emotions, self-contradictions, Feelings Stew.

A List of Feelings

Abused	Cheap	Dubious	Furious
Adamant	Cheated	Dynamic	Gallant
Affable	Childish	Eager	Glad
Affectionate	Clever	Ebullient	Gloomy
Agitated	Combative	Ecstatic	Good
Agonized	Competitive	Edgy	Graceful
Ambivalent	Confused	Electrified	Gratified
Amused	Congenial	Empty	Greedy
Angry	Conspicuous	Enchanted	Grieving
Annoyed	Contented	Energetic	Groovy
Anxious	Contrite	Enervated	Guilty
Apathetic	Cool	Enraged	Gullible
Arrogant	Cordial	Envious	Happy
Ashamed	Crass	Evil	Hateful
Astounded	Cruel	Exasperated	Helpful
Awed	Crushed	Excited	Helpless
Bad	Culpable	Exhausted	High
Bashful	Daring	Exuberant	Homesick
Betrayed	Deceitful	Fabulous	Honored
Bitter	Defeated	Fascinated	Horrible
Blissful	Delighted	Fantastic	Hurt
Bloodthirsty	Desirous	Fearful	Hysterical
Blue	Despairing	Fed up	Ignored
Bold	Destructive	Fierce	Immoral
Bored	Determined	Flattered	Immortal
Bothered	Different	Flustered	Impressed
Brash	Diffident	Foolish	Indifferent
Brave	Diminished	Forlorn	Infatuated
Burdened	Discontent	Freaked	Infuriated
Calm	Distracted	Frustrated	Imposed on
Capable	Distraught	Frightened	Insecure
Captivated	Disturbed	Free	Inspired
Challenged	Dogmatic	Frivolous	Intimidated
Charmed	Divided	Full	Intolerant

Isolated	Mystical	Quirky	Tenacious
Jealous	Nasty	Quixotic	Tender
Jeered	Nauseated	Refreshed	Tense
Jilted	Needy	Rejected	Tentative
Jittery	Nerdy	Relaxed	Terrible
Joyous	Nervous	Relieved	Terrific
Jovial	Numb	Reluctant	Terrified
Jumpy	Nutty	Remorseful	Threatened
Just	Obnoxious	Restless	Thwarted
Keen	Obsessed	Righteous	Trapped
Kind	Obstinate	Robust	Troubled
Kinky	Odd	Rotten	Ugly
Laconic	Offended	Rustic	Uneasy
Languorous	Opposed	Sad	Unheard
Lazy	Ornery	Sanguine	Unsettled
Lecherous	Outraged	Sated	Upset
Left out	Overlooked	Satisfied	Used
Lethargic	Overwhelmed	Scared	Vain
Libeled	Pained	Screwed	Valiant
Licentious	Panicked	Secure	Vigorous
Lonely	Parsimonious	Sexy	Violent
Lousy	Peaceful	Shy	Vitriolic
Lucky	Persecuted	Sickly	Vulnerable
Lustful	Persnickety	Silly	Wicked
Mad	Petrified	Sneaky	Wistful
Marvelous	Pissed off	Solemn	Wondrous
Maudlin	Pitiful	Sorrowful	Worried
Mean	Pleased	Spiteful	Xenophobic
Melancholic	Poetic	Stupid	Yucky
Mocked	Pressured	Subversive	Zany
Moody	Proud	Sympathetic	
Mournful	Put down	Talkative	
Miserable	Quarrelsome	Tempted	

> Do I contradict myself?
>
> Very well then I contradict myself,
>
> (I am large, I contain multitudes.)
>
> Walt Whitman, "Song of Myself," 1855

Another thing that happens with feelings is sudden starts and stops:

- Sam really likes this particular friend one moment, and the next he feels like he can't stand him.
- Gus is totally dedicated to playing trumpet in a casual get-together band. He feels enlivened by it. One day he quits, bored with the band, and begins to spend hours on the computer looking up his family genealogy.
- Marvin is passionately involved with his stocks and bonds until, suddenly, he looses interest and becomes obsessed with his daughter's career in dancing.

As Walt Whitman implies, so what if I contradict myself? Most interesting people do!

Psychologists refer to the feeling of being overwhelmed by emotional distress as "flooding." So if you have moments when you also feel like you're having so many feelings you can't make sense out of them, like you're drowning in Feelings Stew, remember a few things: You're not alone; you're not weird; there is a basis for it in your body. Read on.

Feeling Smart

A new way to understand human intelligence was developed by Dr. Daniel Goleman, a popular psychologist and writer, in his groundbreaking book *Emotional Intelligence*. Goleman points out that we've had a one-sided approach to human intelligence, assuming that it can be completely summed up by our IQ, which is intended to measure our intellectual intelligence. He showed that there is actually is another measure of success in life: emotional intelligence, the ability to relate to feelings intelligently. "In a sense we have two brains, two minds—and two different kinds of intelligence: rational and emotional. How we do in life is determined by both."

Emotional intelligence is "awareness of one's own feelings as they occur"—it is being smart in dealing with your feelings. What a concept!

A lack of emotional intelligence is the reason why some intellectually smart males, of all ages, are not successful; they have an out-of-balance intellectual intelligence and thus can't make their way in an emotionally charged and challenging world. In other words, they are smart knowers but they are not smart feelers. (Like Steve, the guy in my office who screamed, "You sound just like my wife!")

Of course, not all of us are emotional washouts, and each of us has moments of excellence, including you. In fact, the purpose of this book is to provide a simple, specific, and lifelong technique for you to develop emotional intelligence.

Thinking and Feeling

Reason guides but a small part of man, and that the
least interesting. The rest obeys feeling . . ."

—JOSEPH ROUX, FRENCH WRITER

Sometimes feeling is seen as the opposite of thinking: feeling is irrational, emotional, and illogical; thinking is rational, intellectual, and logical; and they never overlap. But a more accurate way to talk about the relationship between thinking and feeling is to see them as seeking balance and as complementary, like friendly allies rather than enemies. Their intertwining is intimate, and they are mutually important for each other.

Feeling can lead to thinking. For example: "I'm really mad and I want to figure out why!" (*Mad* is the feeling part; *figure out* is the thinking part.) And thinking can also lead to feeling. For example: "Jack broke his leg—I'll call and see how he's doing." (*Broken leg* is the thinking fact; *phone call* is the feeling response.)

On the one hand, the feelings we have are often based on the thoughts we have. For example, if I think that a certain breed of dog is dangerous and vicious, I will have feelings of fear when I encounter it. My friend, who raises that breed, does not share my thought and thus feels affection and comfort with the same dog. Our different feelings are based on our different thinking.

On the other hand, we also do a lot of thinking about our feelings. Indeed, it is often our thoughts about feelings that get in our way of identifying and expressing the feelings. If I think tenderness is unmanly, for example, I will tend to kill any tender feelings that may come to me.

Males and females do both. Both are necessary for everyone. Feeling and thinking can coexist in the same sentence ("I think I've got it!"), even in the same word ("Wait!"), yet there are differences.

Thinking is based on rationality and logic and deals with facts, figures, and processes. It is a process that occurs in the part of the brain called the neocortex.

Feeling is based on many differing influences, and it deals with our internal responses and attitudes toward everything. It is a "hearty" process that happens in the portion of the brain called the amygdala.

Thinking is often reasonable and cool, and it attempts to be consistent; it often stays impersonal.

Feeling is typically inconsistent, warm, and spontaneous, and it is invested with your individual values; it tends to take sides and is often intensely personal.

It is instructive to consider the parts of the body we use to talk about each. Thinking comes from the *brain,* operating in the cool, dry, altitude of the *head.* Feeling comes from the lower, warmer, moist regions of the *heart, gut,* and *groin,* and from what has been called our more primitive, or reptilian, brain.

- A thinking kind of statement: "He has a certain attitude that makes it difficult for people to tolerate him."
- A feeling kind of statement: "I don't like that guy."

The first statement distances the speaker from his feelings. The second gets them right out there.

Or put the same sentiments in a positive mode:

- Thinking: "There are certain characteristics about you that I find interesting." (He's keeping what he feels at a safe range.)

- Feeling: "I like you!" (You know where this guy is.)

> **The relationship between feeling and thinking is complementary. They are more like friendly allies than enemies.**

Of course, there are times when you might use the milder statement because of discretion, but you get the idea.

One of the tricks I tried to use when I was in therapy—as the client, not the therapist—was to begin a sentence with "I feel . . ." and then add a thought: "I feel that he's being unfair." My therapist would suggest that that's what I *think*—that he's unfair. Now how do I *feel* about his unfairness? Oh.

There's a special danger for men with a high IQ. It can often lead them to avoid feelings by rationalizing and intellectualizing, which are processes that hide feelings behind ideas in order to avoid the truth to which feelings can lead. Again, this is the difference between intelligence measured by IQ and emotional intelligence. That's what happened to Barry.

■ Barry: A One-Sided Story ■

People with high IQs can be stunningly poor pilots of their private lives.

—DANIEL GOLEMAN, PSYCHOLOGIST

Barry hid behind his intellect for most of his life. It all started with an experience of being deeply shamed at thirteen. He was describing a movie he had seen to a group of friends. He really liked the movie, and his description was colorful, theatrical, and punctuated with dramatic gestures and lines from the movie. He really got into it. But he crossed a line that he was unaware of, and his friends labeled him from that day forward as gay and generally shunned and mocked him.

Barry was very intelligent and he found that intellectual achievement was a way he could get the affirmation that we all seek in order to grow into the adults we want to be. He became a "brain" and kept out all expression of feeling, which was far too dangerous. His intellect led him to considerable achievements, from straight A's and high school valedictorian, to a Ph.D. in chemistry and a teaching position at a prestigious university.

But only at thirty did he begin to open himself to the other side of life. Emotionally he was still about thirteen—scared, hurt, and very well defended. Now, however, he had the personal and social resources to face the other side of his life. He went through a late and abbreviated adolescence and has become a well-rounded, emotionally mature man, who happens to be straight.

There are lots of reasons why we become "one-sided" in

favor of the intellect. The emotional side is messy and can be very challenging, especially if, like Barry, we have an early painful experience. The key here is not to dwell on the reasons why we become one-sided, or even to waste too much time lamenting it, but rather to get on with the process of integration and wholeness.

Feelings Just Are

Are some feelings good and some bad? To put it clearly: they are neither. That's right, feelings—any feeling and all feelings—are neither good nor bad. They are neither blameworthy nor deserving of praise. They are neither immoral nor virtuous. They are not right. They are not wrong.

They just are. That's the first thing to know about your feelings. They just are. This idea is so important that I want to say it in a couple of different ways.

Whatever feelings you have, you cannot be held responsible for the fact of having them. In other words, feelings just come to you on their own. You cannot help feeling what you feel, and you cannot be held responsible for what you have no control over.

To say to yourself, *I shouldn't have this feeling of anger* makes as much sense as saying to yourself, *I shouldn't have these brown eyes.* In both cases, you have no choice. This is one of the key ideas about feelings, so it's important to get it clear.

Of course it is true that feelings can cause either pain or

happiness, and there are some feelings we want and others we try very hard to avoid. There are positive feelings and negative feelings. So you might "feel bad" or "feel good," but the feelings are not bad or good in themselves and *you are not bad or good for having the feelings.*

> **Feelings are not attached to an on-off switch!**

Why do I belabor a point that seems so obvious?

Because so many of us act like we don't understand it. Too often we condemn ourselves just for having negative feelings. And this can lead to a terrible lack of self-esteem and crippling self-hatred, which regularly destroy too many men.

You might feel guilty, for example, when you become aware of feeling hatred or jealousy or wanting to get even, or when your feelings are lusty and sexy. But those feelings just are. They come uninvited, and they cannot be sent packing by a simple act of your will. Feelings are not attached to an on-off switch.

■ Doug's Story: Feeling Grief ■

Grief is a very antisocial state.

—PENELOPE MORTIMER, ENGLISH WRITER

No one should have to go through what Doug went through, especially in so short a time. We all know that change is inevitable, but we can only take so much. Here's his story.

Doug's life was going along just fine. He was happily married, with eighteen-year-old twins, a son and a daughter, who were seniors in high school. Without any warning his wife was diagnosed with cancer. She died only three months after her diagnosis. Within a month of her death, his daughter ran off with her boyfriend to Reno to get married and live there. His son left for college a thousand miles away. Doug's response to all of this was to become emotionally paralyzed.

When friends asked him how he was, he would say that he was fine; he just needed some time. But he was not fine, and time only made things worse. He lost his job. He sold his house and moved in with his wife's sister and her husband in a neighboring city. That's when he came to see me; it was a condition his sister-in-law put on his staying with them.

As he walked into my office, the following things had happened to him within the previous four months: His wife died, his daughter ran off, his son moved away, he lost his job, he sold his house and moved to another city to live with people he didn't particularly like.

And all the time he said he was fine, he just needed some time. He was emotionally overwhelmed and numb. Of course, who wouldn't be?

But no matter what anyone—friends, therapist, relatives—said to Doug about being understanding and patient with himself, he was not. He was very angry with himself and thought, "I should be able to snap out of this and get back to life." He also seemed to blame himself for everything that had happened.

The break came after we had been meeting for a couple months. I said to him, "Doug, why don't you forgive yourself?"

That's what he *said* I said. Frankly, I don't recall saying it. No matter. It's the moment he chose to come out of his fog, whether I actually said it or not. I think he figured that someone heard him and he quite suddenly came back to life. He did "forgive" himself, and then the feelings started to pour out. Tears of grief, anger, frustration, disappointment, resentment, you name it, a real Feelings Stew. But it happened only after he was able to "forgive himself" and accept that he was not guilty for anything that happened. Nor was he guilty for all the angry and revengeful feelings he was now feeling.

Understandable grief—that is, normal grief—over his huge losses had overwhelmed Doug. Too bad he could not have sooner allowed himself permission to feel it and move through it.

Poet and writer on men's issues Robert Bly and others have pointed out that grief is often the first emotional window through which men enter and thus discover our entire emotional life. Our entry into the realm of emotional wholeness is often a result of our losses. Grief is also a feeling that tends to make us challenging to live with, understandably, as the epigraph that begins this section implies.

So feelings come to us whether we want them or not. They just come on their own. Our job is to deal with them, cope with them, live with them, learn from them, and integrate them into our lives.

Moral or Immoral Feelings?

Another way to talk about feelings, especially for those of us who have been influenced by a church, synagogue, or other religious group, is in terms of morality or behavioral norms, that is, the rightness and wrongness of something.

Feelings are neither morally good nor morally bad. They are neither sinful nor virtuous. They are pre-moral. That is, they happen before anything moral or immoral happens. So when you have any feeling, you have not even entered into a moral area yet.

Some religious traditions have a very difficult time with this point. They tend to identify negative feelings with sin. For example, feeling anger is wrong before you even express it, or you are sinful if you feel envious of someone. My point is that nothing immoral (or moral) happens *until* you decide to act, or not act, on your feeling.

Churches often face a challenge in the area of emotions. Indeed, many of them have contributed to and been influenced by the cultural fear of feelings. Typically, churches do not address their members' feeling life at all. Simply stated, most churches are terrified of feelings. Schools and other institutions are no better. I point out these weaknesses not to place blame on churches, but to emphasize that we—you, me, all of us—are a part of a culture that does not have a good track record when it comes to its male members achieving a balanced intelligence.

So: No putting yourself down for having any feeling. And no letting anyone else put you down for any of your feelings.

By the same logic, there's no thinking you're a great gift to the world just because you're feeling generous today.

Deciding and Acting

Of course, this isn't the whole story with feelings. Responsibility and morality certainly *do* enter your feeling life. But, as I said, they enter *only when you decide to act or not to act* on what you feel. At that point you must be accountable to yourself and to the wider community for what you do with the feeling.

Those are the two areas of morality that we humans have to be concerned about: the personal one and the community one. The personal one is your own, individual morality, probably influenced by family, church, friends, and so on. This is the morality that "tells" you if something is right or wrong. It's the morality that forms your conscience.

Law and custom govern the community's morality, which defines what is legal and illegal.

As you decide to act on what you feel, you enter the personal moral realm. So depending on what your decision is—that is, just how you will act out a particular feeling—you will keep or break the standards of your personal morality.

> **Morality, the rightness or wrongness of something, enters the picture only when you *decide* to act (or not to act) on your feelings and then actually carry out your decision.**

Note that the decision is internal to just you, nothing has been "done" yet.

Now as you actually act out what you feel, you enter the second, the community area of morality. Again, you will either keep the community's laws or break them. This is an external act, for which you can be held accountable.

For some, the breaking of personal morality is called sin (telling a serious lie to your spouse); the breaking of community morality is called crime (stealing money). Like the stealing, one event can sometimes be both.

Put Yourself in This Situation: Deciding and Acting

Imagine this: A group has gathered at the watercooler (or its equivalent) at work, and everyone is listening intently to one of the guys. You stand at the edge of the group and listen. It's soon clear that this guy is repeating a story you've already heard. He is telling the group that one of your bosses, a woman you respect and like, is both sexually loose and financially crooked. As your supervisor, she has encouraged you to do your best. You know her to be an honorable woman. She also happens to be a friend of your brother.

As you listen, you are flooded with feelings. The first is *anger.* You feel it mentally as well as physically as your stomach tightens and your teeth clench. You also feel *righteous* as you think of the reputation of this controversial but good supervisor being dragged through the mud. You also feel *fear* at the strong effect of the speaker's words are having on you and what they might lead you to do.

There are other feelings as well: *frustration* at not being able to stop the situation; *disappointment* at the listeners who seem to be agreeing with what they hear; as you listen, your angry feeling might turn into its stronger relative, *rage*.

Let's stop here. Do you see that at this point, for you, nothing moral or immoral has happened yet? You are having a lot of unpleasant feelings, but you have made no decision about them, nor have you acted on them in any way. This is still pre-moral. Now let's look at two possible responses:

Response One: You decide to act on your feelings of anger and frustration by barging into the group of listeners and bashing the offending speaker in the face. All things being equal, I think most would agree you have acted immorally. (Not that this guy wasn't asking for it, but that's not the point, and he was not committing a crime.) And you have acted irresponsibly and can be held accountable to the community for your offence. You have expressed your strong feelings by physical violence and thus have acted both immorally and illegally.

Response Two: Same situation, same feelings. In this scenario you decide to act by speaking out in opposition to the speaker, pointing out the different facts that you know and challenging him to the truth. You get your opinion heard, some of the listeners even agree with you. (This of course is risky; it may hurt your standing at work, but you take the risk.) You have expressed your strong feelings of anger and frustration and have acted responsibly and morally and, of course, legally.

The example is limited, but it may serve to identify situations in which you may confuse the feeling itself with the behavior that expresses the feeling. With both of the above responses you have entered the moral realm because you have both *decided* to act and have *acted.* In the examples, one response was immoral and illegal, the other moral and legal.

Responsibility and accountability do not apply to experiencing the feeling, no matter what the feeling is. They do apply to the decisions and/or actions that result from the feeling.

Wallowing

The Law of Emotional Choice directs us to acknowledge [all] our feelings but also to refuse to get stuck in the negative ones.

—GREG ANDERSON, AMERICAN WRITER

A word about a particular situation: Research shows that while we have no control over a feeling arising, we can, to some extent, influence how long we experience it. So in a certain situation you do have to take responsibility for having feelings: wallowing.

That's when you *wallow* in a negative feeling, so as to *prolong* it; when you *enjoy* your hatred so much that you intentionally *hold onto* it; when you *take shelter* in your jealousy and set up house there; when you *cultivate* your ability to fly into a rage. Or when you *intentionally enter into* situations that will ignite your violence.

The italicized words in the above paragraph indicate acts of your will by which you have brought on or prolonged the feelings. They may have first come on their own, but they have not grown to such proportions on their own. Your encouraging them becomes a behavior for which you are responsible.

I can think of people who seem to love to be frustrated. They search out situations that will frustrate them. In some way, then, they have to take responsibility for having those frustrating feelings because they encourage or seek them out.

What most often gets wallowed in these days, particularly by guys, seems to be the feeling of anger and its by-products: meanness, hostility, rage, and violence. These feelings seem to be both common and troublesome in our stressed-out times.

Our lives are full of frustrating experiences, and anger in many cases is appropriate and even healthy. But too much venting of anger, contrary to some popular belief and practice, can often be harmful. The venting of anger, like pounding a pillow or yelling out loud or throwing and damaging things, can actually increase the intensity of the feeling and cause both physical illness—it can increase the possibility of heart disease, for example—and emotional pain. This can be simply another form of wallowing in the feeling. It's not unusual to hear the encouragement, *C'mon, get your anger out! It's good for you!* While it's good to acknowledge the anger, it's now clear that too much "getting it out" can make it worse.

Of course wallowing in positive feelings that everyone enjoys—like *eagerness, satisfaction,* and *enthusiasm*—is no problem. It can in fact be helpful to stretch out these feelings, spread them around, so to speak. Unfortunately for many of us, we often run from happiness and wallow in anger.

A Few Suggestions for Review

- Go back to the List of Feelings on pages 36–37 and read it over. Are there any that you are particularly attracted to? Uncomfortable with? If there are some words you are unfamiliar with, take a moment and look them up in a dictionary.

- Put a check by some of the feelings you have known and briefly recall the circumstances of the experience. Or, at the top of the List of Feelings page write the name of an intensely emotional event from your life, then underline all the different feelings you experienced at that time.

- Can you think of a time when you have "wallowed" in a feeling? Is there a particular negative feeling that you're sometimes tempted to prolong or encourage?

- Sometime soon, tell someone you like and trust that you are reading this book and how it's affecting you.

three

Damages and Differences

I hope it is clear that when we do not deal intelligently with the emotional life, it causes us trouble. The very part of life that can bring depth and joy, often brings us serious damages instead. And then there are the differences: between individuals and between men and women. Here the focus is on getting rid of the damages and understanding the differences.

■ Zack's Story ■

Now I want to introduce you to Zack. He's not a client; he's a friend. He is just one example of the American man of the early twenty-first century, but I believe he represents parts of many of us. Zack describes himself as "dangerously close to forty and plunging into midlife with a certain amount of dread."

He's been married for ten years and has an eight-year-old son. Zack is very successful at his job at a large consulting firm. He told me that all he has to do is say the word and he gets everything he wants or needs from the company to do his work. So he's a successful man on the moon, to use our metaphor; he's got the thinking, technical, logical part down pat, even though he doesn't like his job and often feels bored and unsatisfied.

He and his wife have a "fairly good" marriage, according to him. Wilma, his wife, gives it lower marks. They seem to be growing apart recently. Their sex life is lackluster, and each of them pursues different interests, coming together mostly around parenting their son.

Zack has friends with whom he plays racquetball and a few drinking buddies. But he and Wilma don't have much of a social life. They also quit going to church, but Zack keeps the moral attitudes he got from his parents growing up.

Zack is one of those people everyone calls a "really nice guy"—and he is. He tries to be fair and decent to people. He's a regular, friendly guy. But he's not happy, not really. Life is dull for him; nothing seems to really pique his interest. He feels passionless and has nothing to look forward to. He has no enthusiasm or interest in his work.

So one Friday evening he's giving me a lift home and he is in a down mood. I can tell by his erratic driving and by the way he's jumpy and nervous, which he frequently is. I can also tell by the way he stares into space and doesn't talk much—even though I know he wants to talk. He keeps starting sentences, "You know . . . it's . . . I think if I . . ." but not finishing them.

Being a family counselor, I tend to notice these things. So I can tell Zack wants to talk, but he doesn't say anything, which is OK with me because I have been in my office all day with people who want to talk and I'm tired.

But I'm feeling a little bad for him, so I say, "Zack, what's wrong?"

"Nothing's wrong, I'm fine," he answers.

Oh, great, I think. *He sits there jumpy and nervous, silent and surly, with a hung-dog look, muttering away, and says nothing's wrong.* So when we get to my place I quickly jump out saying, "See ya, Zack. Thanks for the ride." Like I said, I was tired.

When I'm feeling better, I recall past conversations with Zack when he told me he often feels anxious. He occasionally has mild anxiety attacks (he doesn't call them that) like an upset feeling that overtakes him, especially when he is stressed or tired; he breaks into a sweat, and even shakes a little. He gets nervous when he is in a confined space and has trouble falling asleep. He told me once he "tried to talk" to a woman friend of his, but she responded by telling him all *her* problems.

I know that Zack senses something is wrong but he can't put his finger on it. He doesn't know what's wrong. Unlike Steve, the guy who yelled at me, Zack is not facing a crisis in his marriage, nor in any other part of his life. He's "got it good," as he says.

It's true, Zack has a lot going for him—basically good health, a bright, attractive wife who is concerned about him, enough money, a job, sufficient education, a good personality, his son is a good kid. But something is missing. I think he's also embarrassed that he can't figure it out for himself.

By changing the circumstances—his age, the symptoms of

his anxiety attacks, and other minor details—you can find men like Zack everywhere. There are millions of them.

So what is going on with Zack? Why is he mildly depressed, bored, and isolated? I think I know the answer to that question. I think—no, I know—it's because he wouldn't recognize a feeling even if he tripped over it. Like Jim, Derek, and Steve, he too has trouble identifying and expressing what he is feeling.

He is so removed from his feelings, and thus from the ability to express them, that he is missing life's most rewarding moments, moments that could bring him their own unique pleasures, as well as connect him, by intimacy, to the lives of others.

Love to Work? Work to Love?

Most men have pursued excellence as breadwinners, work machines, and performers, and everything else in their lives has suffered.

—Gary Oliver, psychologist

The key for Zack, and for millions of other men, is the strong influence of his work on his personal life. He is very focused on his work, and it seems to control his life. The message at most workplaces is clear: Don't let what you personally feel have any place at work. The assumption is that a man's feeling life should be confined to his home and to his family and not brought to work. The problem with this arrangement is that it doesn't work very well.

I don't deny the necessities of the workplace; rules and boundaries are necessary. A man should not let his personal feelings hurt his work or get in the way of his work; he must strive for objectivity and relevance. What is unacceptable—as well as harmful to productivity—is for a man, whether at work or at home, to have no feeling life at all.

In order to survive, many of us develop two different dispositions, or temperaments, as it were, two different expressions of our personality for the two different parts of our lives. We have one for work and another for home. The work temperament is efficient, stoic, and coolly humorous; it avoids feelings. The home temperament is warm, playful, spontaneous, and more inclusive of feelings. Frequently neither one is as well developed as it could be, and even more frequently the two never "meet."

It is difficult to change back and forth between temperaments as you daily trek from home to work. Turn off your feelings as you go to work, turn on your feelings as you come home. It's just damn hard to do that. In fact, the very structure of human brains, specifically the relationship between the neocortex and the amygdala, makes this a strenuous, if not impossible, task. Many just give in, like Zack, without making a clear decision. The work temperament wins out, and the feelings never find a place of their own.

The reasons for this, conscious or not, are understandable.

After all, to survive we have to work. Call it the "economic imperative." But we don't *have* to have a home life; we think we can scrimp on that and at least survive. Another reason is that we tend to feel less pain in the work mode; at least we are more adept at hiding and denying work-originated pain. Of course, at the same time, we hide ecstasy and joy as well. Also, from very early in our industrial history, the financial rewards for hard work have been considerable; many men have experienced a high degree of achievement in their work and have been rewarded with position and influence. It's hard not to be swayed by money, power, and success.

So the goal here—and the challenge for Zack—is to make it an issue not of "either/or" but of "both/and." You are not *either* a worker *or* a lover, but *both* one who works *and* one who loves—a loving worker, a working lover. It is not a matter of separation but of *integration*.

Workaholism

Workaholism is defined as compulsive, out-of-control working.

Workaholism is a unique offering to the world from the rugged individualism of industrialized society.

The world of business has given birth to a creature, the workaholic, more perfectly designed to assure its own continued existence—or so it seems—than it had ever intended.

Your working and home temperaments always have access to each other, so to speak; both are merely different expressions of your one personality. But because this is difficult, from both the physiological and psychological point of view, you have to make an intentional decision to integrate your two modes of living. That integration consists of knowing and being able to express in some appropriate way what you are feeling at any given moment, which is the goal of this book.

Buried Alive

Much of the trouble happens when we bury our feelings, when we just pretend they're not there. Thus, the very first and vitally important thing you have to do in dealing with any feeling is really something that you must *not* do. Don't bury it. Don't run from it and don't cover it over. Just stay in the moment and feel it.

Just feel it.

Don't bury. Don't run. Don't cover.

Just stay with it for a while, be aware of it. Acknowledge it, which is like saying "Oh, it's you" to the feeling. Got the idea? Just stay put; don't run. Just feel.

Now it's one thing to do this when you're feeling excited or flattered. It's another thing when you're feeling mad or lonely. Who wants to acknowledge or stay with those feelings? Nobody wants to, but all those who are successful with feelings, do. Feel angry. Feel lonely.

It doesn't seem right, but it is. If you stay with the negative feeling, at least for a while, you will resolve it sooner and more completely. And when you stay with the positive feelings, the enjoyment increases.

What gets you into trouble is when you are feeling angry, for instance, and you say to yourself, "No, I'm not angry! Who? Me? Angry? Naah." Why does this lead to trouble?

It's troublesome because if you do not stay with the feeling, if you deny it, or run from it, then the feeling won't have a chance to tell you how to express it, how to get it out. And if it doesn't get out, it's buried. And if it's buried, *it's always buried alive!*

"Buried alive" means that the feeling is never expressed. To be expressed is what a feeling craves; it's a feeling's reason for being. A fish swimming, a bird flying, and a feeling expressed are three things that are alike.

When the feeling is buried alive, it never finds its own life. Rather, it's stuffed away and ignored before it has the chance to do what it was meant to do—get expressed.

The energy created by that buried feeling, like any energy, cannot disappear; it has to do something or go somewhere. Because the feeling is frustrated, the energy it generates is strong and desperate. Have you ever held a fish out of water or kept a bird from flying? That's what the energy is like. The feeling is literally fighting for its life. The only difference is that the feeling never dies. Never.

The Damage

> By starving emotions we become humorless and rigid . . .
> by repressing them we become literal . . . and holier-
> than-thou; encouraged, they perfume life; discouraged, they
> poison it.
>
> —JOSEPH COLLINS, BIBLICAL SCHOLAR

What happens when feelings are not expressed in a healthy way by their owner? They do damage. While it may be true that very mild or minor feelings tend to fade away on their own, the important ones don't.

The first fact to understand is that they *will* come out on their own, possibly without you knowing what they are as they come out. This unintentional expression can take at least three forms, none of them desirable: The first possibility is addictive behavior, such as problem drinking or eating. The second possibility is that they turn on their owner in a bodily way, like a mad dog, and cause physical sickness. The third is emotional or mental illness.

Am I saying that unexpressed or buried feelings can actually cause serious afflictions like alcoholism and cancer and depression? Yes. Let's look at addictions first.

Addictions

An addiction is any process or substance that we have no power to control. An addiction is using, doing, or being something that is not what we really want and that we cannot stop. Many of us are addicted.

Those addicted to narcotic drugs and alcohol may be more obvious than others, but some are addicted to other substances such as nicotine and caffeine. Still others are addicted to processes such as accumulating money, gambling, sex, work, religion, worry, and so on. We can be addicted to anything.

Sometimes the difference between really liking something and being addicted is a fine line indeed. Don't be overly hard on yourself. Passionate care for something is often misdiagnosed as an addiction. Common sense, the feedback of a good friend, and, if necessary, professional input, can generally resolve the difference between an addiction and just liking something very much and doing it a lot.

■ Pete's Story ■

What is the connection between buried feelings and addictions? Often buried feelings are the *cause* of addictions. It's that simple. To illustrate, let's take a common situation, a drinking problem.

This is a story of a young gay man, Pete. He's twenty-eight and is bombarded by feelings. He and his partner of two years have just decided to move in together and make a commitment to each other (his feelings: *excited, happy, fulfilled*). But soon after, he notices his partner becoming more distant and withdrawn (his feelings: *caring, lonely, afraid, confused*).

There are problems at work with his boss (feelings: *fearful, frustrated*) and with some of his coworkers (feelings: *resentful, angry, envious*).

His youngest brother was just named football player of the year of his college (feelings: *proud, enthusiastic, happy*), and a close friend was in the hospital two days recently as a result of severe headaches of unknown cause (feelings: *worried, anxious, helpless*).

He has recently noticed a growing anxiety about his financial situation (feelings: *scared, embarrassed*). And so on and so forth. This is just normal life, nothing unusual here.

Pete has all these feelings that are begging for his attention. There are twenty-some feelings mentioned above, and these are just a few of the many in any given day or week of his life. But he is unable to acknowledge them, to identify them, or to express them. There are many men who would not recognize that they were having any feelings at all.

The pressure and pain of these buried feelings lead Pete to search for relief. In the short run, he finds alcohol relieves the pressure and lessens the pain. Alcohol depresses the central nervous system, so it lowers inhibition. He is more relaxed, and he can even express some of his feelings. In the long run, however, alcohol fosters depression. It is also an addicting substance. People like Pete can become addicted without even knowing it.

Addictions have a purpose, even though it's a lousy one: They shut off, block out, and bury feelings that we believe we cannot handle, such as fear, envy, anger, anxiety, panic, and rage. They can even destroy joy, excitement, pleasure, and happiness.

Whether or not you think you have, or will have, a problem with addictive behavior, I encourage you to get information about alcohol and addictions. You deserve to have this knowledge, and it could be vitally important to you and others in your life, especially if you're a parent. James R. Milam and Katherine Ketcham's book, *Under the Influence* (listed in the bibliography) is a place to start.

Pete's way out was his dedicated involvement in the twelve-step program of Alcoholics Anonymous (AA).

Physical Illness

Another possibility, when you do not express feelings in a healthy way, is that you become sick. In this case, the feelings turn in, as it were, and begin to attack you.

The longer the feelings remain buried, the more damage to the person. Symptoms can continue for many years. They can begin in small ways such as back pain, stomachache, or sore throat and can end in heart disease and cancer. I am not saying that buried feelings cause all illnesses. I am saying that they cause many, and can make all illnesses worse.

■ Jack's Secret ■

Jack is in his late fifties and he is carrying within himself a secret in the form of some very well-buried feelings. In Jack's case, it is a dirty and reckless deed of his early life. (With another it may be something that causes great shame, perhaps an unresolved and hurtful family relationship that produces hate and resentment, maybe a feeling of guilt and embarrassment. The possibilities are endless.)

Jack has never expressed this secret—this complex of feelings—to any other human being, ever. In his twenties and early thirties, the symptoms of stress hardly affected him, just frequent difficulties with his lower gastrointestinal tract, which he endured stoically. Now, in his later middle-age, he has developed intestinal polyps, and his doctor has just told him that they are precancerous.

The inexorable effect of unrelieved stress on the human organism, like the slow, grinding movement of a glacier on the earth, is to wear it down. Jack is now facing life-threatening cancer. The ultimate cause of that cancer is that buried secret.

Emotional Illness

There are a lot of sad guys out there.

—SABIN RUSSELL, JOURNALIST

What do Prime Minister Winston Churchill, President Abraham Lincoln, writer William Styron, and artist Mark Rothko have in common? They all suffered from serious depression, as do many men. And the most salient fact about men who are depressed is that a large percentage of them don't do anything about it. Why?

Men are "ashamed about being ashamed, depressed about being depressed," says Terrence Real, author of *I Don't Want to Talk about It: Overcoming the Secret Legacy of Male Depression,* so they become stoic. "But Stoicism kills. We don't raise boys to be intimate, we raise them to be good, competitive perform-ers. But competitive men can be inwardly lonely and empty. The ultimate cure for depression is intimacy," says Real.

Another fact: Treating depression is one of psychiatry's successes. Real reports that "ninety percent of men and women who are treated for depression report substantial relief."

21st Century Emotional Challenges

Every age has its emotional challenges. Here are some that seem to be particularly common at the beginning of the twenty-first century:

Anxiety

Addictions

Depression

Eating Disorders

Bi-Polar (manic-depressive) Disorder

Adult Children of Alcoholics Syndrome (ACA)

Post-traumatic Stress Disorder (PTSD)

Attention Deficit Disorder (ADD)

Hyperactivity

If depression touches you personally, resolve to do something about it. At least, please read Real's excellent book mentioned above.

Indeed if any emotional distress affects you, consider therapy. Understand that once your emotional system has learned something, your mind resists letting it go. What therapy can do is teach you to name it and express it. In physiological terms, it teaches your neocortex how to inhibit your amygdala, an up-hill battle, simply based on the structure of the brain.

Now a suggestion. Ask yourself a question here: *Do I really believe that buried feelings can cause my serious illnesses?*

There is a tendency to chalk this stuff up to psychologists who talk psychobabble or doctors who don't know what else to do with their time. It would be a serious mistake to do that. It would also be a dumb mistake, because it would deny you information that you, a man of the twenty-first century, deserve to have.

The way in which buried feelings finally have their way with you is not always an either/or proposition: either they lead you to addictions or emotional illness *or* they attack your body. Often it is a *both/and* situation: they cause you *both* emotional *and* physical symptoms, a double whammy you don't need.

Murderous Boys, Violent Men

Depression is rage spread thin.

—Paul Tillich, German-American theologian

Some of the Signs of Depression

- Feeling sad, irritable, or empty

- Loss of interest in pleasure or in things you once enjoyed

- Weight gain or loss, over- or undereating

- Changes in patterns of sleep

- Feeling guilty or without hope

- Inability to concentrate, remember, or make decisions

- Significant loss of energy

- Others notice your lack of energy

- Thoughts of suicide or death

Especially if you have several (3–5) of these symptoms over a period of time (two weeks) look into getting help. Help works!

Killing rampages by school boys, teenagers who murder their parents, husbands who beat their wives and children, snipers who pick off people like tin cans; we really don't have to be reminded of the pervasive presence of male violence in our society. It appears every day.

The presence of so much male violence is perhaps the clearest sign that the emotional education and skills that we men have received are failing us badly.

In their excellent book *Raising Cain: Protecting the Emotional Life of Boys,* Dan Kindlon and Michael Thompson say this: "The difference between boys who turn violent and those who don't is that the violent ones lack sufficient psychological resources to control their emotional reactions." By extension, we can include adult males in the same category.

Nothing's Wrong is based on the strong conviction that there is a direct and causal relationship between violent behavior in males and their repressed (buried) feelings. Remember, feelings will come out one way or another. When anger and resentment grow into enough powerful energy that can no longer be contained, the result is often immense destruction and devastation.

The buried feelings are the cause of the violence.

Think of a furnace. Fuel pumped into the furnace is burned to create energy, heat. The heat is pumped out through ducts to accomplish its purpose, to heat the house. It's an efficient and useful cycle: fuel pumped in, energy pumped out. What happens when the fuel is pumped in and burned but the ducts are blocked and no energy flows out? The furnace explodes. You get the picture.

Here's the way it needs to work: Events of life are pumped into you as fuel. You have reactions, or feelings, about these events (and people, and situations, etc.). Then you pump them out into the world where they accomplish their purpose, to connect you in a real and healthy way with your world and the people in it. This process is, in essence, the Three Steps to Emotional Fitness, which we'll explore in detail.

Men and Women: Guts and Hearts

> The test of a man is how well he is able to feel about what he thinks. The test of a woman is how well she is able to think about what she feels.
>
> —MARY MCDOWELL, D. 1936, LABOR ORGANIZER

Most people probably believe that women are, always have been, and always will be more naturally adept at the emotional life than men. It's one of the ways men and women are different from one another. Indeed, many studies have shown that women's brains are wired differently from men's so they can both feel and recall both positive and negative emotions more strongly than men.

The crucial point to understand here is that just because women seem to be more comfortable in the emotional realm, does not mean that men don't, can't, or shouldn't thrive in it. There is a man's way to do it. It's just sometimes not the same as a woman's way. In place of being judged as deficient, let us merely be understood as different.

The differences between us have been, in fact, part of our problem. For the most part, we've been trying to learn from teachers with only part of the information we need: women—our mothers, sisters, wives, partners, and friends. It's not that we can't learn feelings from women; I believe we can. I also believe we cannot learn *everything* we need to know from women, which is understandable because of our differences. It's certainly not their fault; they teach what they know. But too often we learn skills that don't serve us well, so we abandon them, along with an attempt to find our own. In addition, our fathers were often not there to teach us more useful skills; nor were their fathers. This has been going on for a long time.

What brings about these differences between men and women? Do we learn them from our experience (nurture)? Or are they inborn (nature)? Or, the position of most people, is it a combination of both? Now this is a very tricky area, and I will try to resist strict definitions and conclusions. Who, after all, can really understand these differences?

But having said that, I believe there are certain ways we tend to differ, generally speaking, from women in our emotional life.

The Differences

To attempt to understand the differences in the ways men and women feel, we have to understand the importance of their learned roles. Here I use the word role to mean what society expects, stereotypically, from men and women and, especially, what society does not expect.

We might describe a man's role as rational, aggressive, and practical. Men take care of "Thinking," "War," and "Fixing Things." We have different expectations of a woman. Traditionally, her role could be described as emotional, nurturing, and creative. Women take care of "Feeling," "Kids," and "Decorating." So the expression of feelings will flow from these roles that we receive from our culture and will carry the culture's changing and tension-filled biases and preferences as they are expressed—*generally* speaking.

Carried to an extreme, which it sometimes is, these exclusive roles produce both men and women who live a sad half-life; the woman does no thinking; the man, no feeling.

Something to note about these roles: The differences between the sexes are important and necessary. To ignore them would be folly. As the French remind us, *Vive la différence!* however large or small those differences may be. It's the exclusiveness of the roles and their exaggeration that are troublesome. The roles are stereotypes, oversimplifications, so they are not hard and fast; there are many exceptions and reversals. To act as if only women are nurturing and only men are aggressive, or only women are good at decorating and only men can fix things is nonsense.

So men and women are not the same. Thinking that we are the same—that there are no differences at all, even general and stereotypical ones—gets us into problems of communication and getting along. Men *are* from Mars and women *are* from Venus, as John Gray's popular book of the same name reminds us.

However, as Gray is careful to point out, there is a problem when you speak in terms of being from different planets. It can lead you into a popular misconception: Men and women are polar opposites. This attitude leads us too frequently into blame: Women are wonderful; men are jerks! Or men have it all together; it's women who cause the problems!

In his book *Real Men Have Feelings, Too*, psychologist Gary Oliver talks about a third way: "Are men and women different? Most definitely! Are all of those differences genetic? No. Are many of the differences cultural? Yes. Are men and women opposites? No." So we don't have to be better or worse. We don't have to be polar opposites. We are just often very different from one another, and some of our differences are not based on gender, but simply on the fact that we are different people.

Flooding

Daniel Goleman cites research by John Gottman that says men get to a "flooding" stage—a feeling of being overwhelmed by feelings—much more quickly than do women. And once men are flooded, they secrete more adrenaline into their bloodstream, and unlike women, it then takes very little negativity on the part of someone they're arguing with, for example, to greatly increase the adrenaline and thus reinforce the overwhelmed feeling. It also takes us longer to recover from this feeling. Goleman suggests perhaps "the stoic, Clint Eastwood type of male imperturbability may represent a defense against feeling emotionally overwhelmed."

This may well be why men are often accused of "stonewalling," or withdrawing and becoming unresponsive in the face of strong emotions by others. It prevents the flooding from happening so we can move on more easily and take care of whatever practical needs we have to deal with.

Talking about It

> A study in the *Washington Post* says that women have better
> verbal skills than men. I just want to say to the authors of
> that study: "Duh."
>
> —CONAN O'BRIEN, TALK-SHOW HOST

One of the specific differences that I want to mention is "talking about it." Often, women want to talk about feelings, hers as well as ours, and, well, often we'd really rather not talk about it. This, of course, is also based on the physiology of the brain. Girls develop a facility with language earlier and stronger than boys. They tend to keep that edge throughout life. Conan O'Brien's glib comment above says it all.

A man's response to a woman's *talking about it* is often to "fix it," that is to do or say something that will take care of the feeling, when all she wants is to be heard and accepted. From a woman's point of view, it can feel like you are cutting her off, avoiding her feelings, and jumping to solutions—something she's not interested in—*yet.*

When this happens, try to remember three things: First, women are more comfortable with conflict than we are; their brains are made that way. So we almost always think their emotion—anger, upset, fear, frustration, whatever—is worse than it really is. Second, they get over it more quickly than we do. So just hang in there a while and it will pass. Third, and most important, don't think you have to help her stop the feeling or offer her a solution to any feeling; simply listen and somehow show that you understand (even if you don't really) and accept that that's what she's feeling.

Then, after the accepting, let your skills with answers and solutions have their day. The acceptance of a feeling can be as simple as saying, "Yes, I can understand that you feel that way."

Lastly, at these moments of noticing and talking, don't forget to breathe. Two or three deep breaths will help, probably a lot more than you'd expect.

From the Gut: A Man's Way to Feel

> While we can deceive ourselves (by mislabeling what we are feeling and downplaying the intensity of the emotion), basically we tend to be the expert of what we are feeling.
>
> —D. BRADFORD AND M. HUCKABAY,
> STANFORD BUSINESS SCHOOL

What are some of the specific ways that the world sees men as different from women in the expression of feelings? We might begin, as I mentioned in the introduction, with an overall description of men as feeling "from the gut" and women as feeling "from the heart." That begins to set the tone for the differences. "Gut" carries feelings of spontaneity and power; "heart" of caring and gentleness.

There are many ways of describing these differences, and every commentator seems to have favorites. Here are eight stereotypes or qualities of "feeling from the gut" that I have

culled from many. These seem to be the dominant characteristics of the way men, specifically, deal with feelings. See if they
ring true for you:

1. We tend to be aggressive, rather than passive, favoring
   what many see as the "typically masculine" approach.

2. Related to that, we favor competitive feelings with firm
   expression, rather than cooperative feelings with gentle
   expression, a tendency that certainly has deep roots in
   the culture in which we were raised, and perhaps an
   historical remnant from the ancient male role of
   hunter/provider.

3. We like to be literal, rather than symbolic, so while we
   sometimes miss symbolic or nonverbal emotional
   expressions—a sigh, a smile, a gesture, an absence—
   we're good at picking up literal and physical signs.

4. We favor logic rather than emotion as a motive for acting,
   and thus will often be moved to do something based
   on a rational, not an emotional, process.

5. We often get to an emotion by way of a thought, rather
   than directly to the emotion. Often our first response
   to anything is thinking about it or acting upon it. Feeling
   follows.

6. Similarly, our preference is to express a feeling by an
   action—doing something, such as enjoying an activity
   together with a spouse or a friend—rather than by talking about it.

7. We typically express feelings infrequently, rather than

often, leading some to judge wrongly that sometimes we don't *have* feelings.

8. We tend to favor feelings that foster a sense of independence, rather than a sense of connectedness to others.

But do you see the problem here? For every one of those eight stereotypes, I—and surely you—can name people in whom the stereotypes are reversed. It's the very nature of a stereotype to be oversimplified and uncritical. I know of relationships in which the man has more nurturing energy than the woman; and in others, the woman has more aggressive and competitive energy than the man. There are same-sex couples whose combined parenting skills, for example, cover all the bases.

Also, please don't see the characteristics listed above as negative in any way, or as positive, for that matter. I'm sure I indicate my own attitude when I use many qualifying expressions in this section, such as "perhaps," "tend to," "often prefer," "favor," and such.

Author Deborah Tannen makes an important point in her book *Please Understand Me:* "What may be the subtlest yet deepest source of frustration and puzzlement arising from the different ways that women and men approach the world is that we [all] feel we know how the world is, and we look to others to reinforce that conviction. When we see others acting as if the world were an entirely different place from the one we inhabit, we are shaken."

Do you remember *The Honeymooners* on TV (or the re-runs)? Might this be the motivation for Jackie Gleason's character, Ralph Cramden, who, when he was frustrated and angry, would point to the sky and yell at his wife, "To the moon, Alice!"

So what does all this mean? How does a man feel? I believe it comes down to this: The way a man feels is the way *you* feel right now, in *this* situation, with *your* background and *your* experience. That's how a man feels. If it's different from a women, fine. If it's similar, fine. That is not important. It's what you are in fact feeling that's important.

Robert Jensen, writing in the September/October 2002 issue of *Clamor* magazine, seems to have this idea in mind when he says, "I have never met a man who didn't feel uneasy about masculinity, who didn't feel that in some way he wasn't living up to what it means to be a man. There's a reason for that: Masculinity is a fraud; it's a trap. None of us are man enough." In other words, the popular idea of masculinity is not based on reality, but on, perhaps, a collective and oversimplified wish or an unrealistic and historically influenced dream.

> **How does a man feel? The way a man feels is the way *you* feel right now, in *this* situation, with *your* history and experience, with *your* response to this moment. *That's* how a man feels!**

There is no hidden and predetermined form of masculinity waiting in some dark corner for us to find it. There is no "secret way" out there that you need to discover, or an "eternal practice" somewhere that you must constantly seek in order to know how to feel like a man. No. What *you* feel is what and how a *man* feels!

We will take up more about the particular way of expressing emotions when we deal with the Three Steps to Emotional Fitness in chapter 4. Just how you express what you are feeling is, of course, going to be affected by many influences, such as your personal preferences, your style, experiences, and history.

Dealing with Feminism

Feminism has brought about big changes in the way women see themselves and their roles. I believe we must admit that, on the whole, we are behind on that score. Women have embraced their guts; have we embraced our hearts? (For the sake of clarity, Webster's Collegiate Dictionary defines *feminism* as "the theory of the . . . equality of the sexes" and "organized activity on behalf of women's rights and interests.")

Now—and this is of great and practical importance—to ignore or to deny the changes that women have accomplished in the last thirty years puts a man in a weakened position. Such an attitude is not based on facts, and it makes us less interesting and less successful.

Whether to agree with all, or some, or none of the issues of the feminist movement is *not* the point. You don't have to agree with anything. But simply to mock feminism is to buy directly into the deception that keeps us half alive.

In her book *Heart of Flesh,* author Joan Chittister describes the serious harm that our opposing or making fun of feminism does to men. She says, simply, it is "killing" us. It's killing us—males—because it sets up a goal impossible to accomplish. Life for men in a world that relegates women to an unequal and lower status becomes one long struggle to stay in charge, whatever the cost.

> **To mock feminism is to buy directly into the deception that keeps us half alive.**

We are trained to be aggressive, so we know the cost of having to "prove ourselves" over and over again. And we also know the pain of being hazed, beat up, and sneered at, and of having our courage confused with weakness. Our feelings are denied, says Chittister, and in their place we can "look forward to heart attacks and alcoholism."

What do girls and women want? I believe the majority of them want boys and men who are *both* strong and protective *and* sensitive and feeling. They want us to be both the astronaut and the man in the moon.

The Way We Are: Cowboys and Executives

Men aren't the way they are because they want to drive women crazy; they've been trained to be that way for thousands of years.

—BARBARA DE ANGELIS, PSYCHOLOGIST, WRITER

Certainly there are reasons why we're the way we are. You can find them throughout our history. Here are three hundred years of our history jammed into four points:

One: Puritans, 1700s

- Didn't like authority
- Wanted to purify the Church
- Were suspicious of Catholics
- Believed work more important than fun

Two: Settlers of the West, 1800s

- Tamed the wilderness
- Found hardship everywhere
- Drove out native peoples
- Became cowboys and ranchers

Three: Workers, 1900s

- Built factories of the Industrial Revolution
- Became businessmen/executives

- Became managers and workaholics
- Went to the moon

Four: Space—Outer and Cyber, 2000s

- Sit at computers
- ?
- ?

On every line in the above history, and especially between the lines, you can find cultural reasons why males have not done so well with the feeling part of life. They had work to do. And gradually work became separated from home. Head and heart split. And it's that split that we're trying to put back together now.

But let's face it, the cowboy was—and is still?—the ideal hero: strong, unbreakable, unfeeling, and, finally, alone. Think of them: Shane, the Cartwrights . . . wandering off alone into the sunset.

Many of the usual traits of the historically "typical male," such as strength, self-reliance, and forcefulness, are just fine. Not fine is what tends to tag along with them, like loneliness, isolation, and depression.

The Puritan would have been fully alive if he could have seen not only the seriousness of life but also its whimsy and humor, its spontaneity and joy.

The cowboy would be fully alive if he could, at the end of his chores, walk off into the sunset *with* someone.

The executive would be fully alive if he could meet the challenge to bring together his heart (home and family) and his head (work) and become the same person in both places.

Different Histories

I want to acknowledge that many North American men are part of a different history. The history of Native American and First Nations men, certainly, is different. Men of Asian, African, and Hispanic culture; gay and bisexual men; and other national or cultural or social groups—such as the men of Mexico and Central America and the Francophone peoples of Canada—come from traditions that could be different from, or similar to, the tradition and history of the majority of the United States and Canada: straight, white, European.

Indeed, all males of whatever ethnic origins, cultural groupings, or sexual orientations will do well to drink deeply from the waters of each other's richly unique emotional heritage. Such refreshment will nurture us all.

The beginning of the twenty-first century is what many see as the end of an industry-based society. We are becoming an information-based society dominated by computers, communications systems, and robots. And again, new roles for men.

But the poet David Whyte leads us to a deeper truth, as poets often do: this isn't *really* the age of information:

Loaves and Fishes

This is not
the age of information.

This is *not*
the age of information.

Forget the news,
and the radio,
and the blurred screen.

This is the time
of loaves
and fishes.

People are hungry,
and one good word is bread
for a thousand.

—DAVID WHYTE FROM *THE HOUSE OF BELONGING*

I believe the "good word" that we each can express and
that serves as "bread" for others—the actual word or words will
of course be different for all of us—will be motivated by deeply
felt emotions. Thus, I am hopeful that a society dominated by
the computer, ironically, will be the society in which American
men will finally integrate their heads and their hearts. We need
to take back what is rightfully ours from the moment of birth:
the ability to live both aspects of our lives as fully, as freely, and
as completely as we want and need.

The Big Lie

From the moment of birth, boys and girls are taught that there are some things we are expected to be and some things we are not. Little boys can be aggressive; little girls cannot. Boys are strong; girls shouldn't be too strong. Boys don't cry when they hurt; it's OK for little girls. Boys play baseball; girls play house. The list is endless, and each of us could add his own particular items.

When as children we experimented outside our roles, we were often made to adapt by powerful teachers: shame and scorn.

The little girl playing baseball or expecting to be taught the same life skills as her brothers is called a tomboy. The little boy who prefers books to sports or wants to learn ballet with his sister is called a sissy. Do you notice something right away? It's this: little girls outside their roles are much more acceptable to society than are little boys outside theirs. Even though recently many of these attitudes are changing, it remains true: tomboys we can deal with; sissies make us uncomfortable.

What's the worst thing one thirteen-year-old boy can say to another? Isn't it something like, "You're a big sissy" or "You're just a fag" or "You're just like a girl!" So think for a moment, what are both thirteen-year-olds learning in that exchange? Isn't it that *to be* anything like a girl is bad? So they both think *I must do everything I can to not be like a girl!* So they stop what is seen as a feminine trait. They stop feeling.

But no! They don't stop feeling! Remember, feelings just

are and they don't go away. What they stop is *expressing* their feelings. They begin to bury them, and so begin their sad journey to a frustrated, unhappy half-life.

The scorn and shame felt by boys for being out of their roles is devastating. They say to the boy: There is something wrong with the way you are, and he very quickly learns never to let that feeling show again. But, of course, the feeling or the desire doesn't go away. It just gets buried. And as we've already seen, these buried feelings often come out on their own in the form of addictions or illnesses.

> **The Big Lie:**
> **"For a male to show**
> **feelings is weakness."**

Please understand that the roles and the differences are not bad. I believe it is good to teach boys bravery and girls gracefulness. Even to emphasize certain roles for each can be helpful. But it is positively harmful and unfair to make these roles exclusive and unbending and to induce shame when the child's natural inclinations lead him or her to expand beyond the stereotypes. It is also good to teach boys gracefulness and girls bravery.

Yes, men have been told lies. If I were to condense the lies into The Big Lie, it would be this: "For a male to show feelings is weakness." That's a big lie because it robs us of half our life.

It's important to say here that the people who lied to us did not do it on purpose. Families and teachers were teaching only what their families and teachers taught them. That's the tragedy of systems that have become unhealthy, the lie gets passed from one generation to another, from one system to another, until finally somebody stops it by telling the truth.

Schools and churches have lied to us in the same way. We are told: Good boys don't cheat (or steal or lie or talk when they shouldn't or throw tantrums or think about sex or bite other children or . . .) But what we hear is: Good boys don't do this, but I do this, so I am not good. This process produces shame, an impossible basis for self-acceptance and self-understanding. No less a teacher than Paul says it clearly: "Be angry, and yet do not sin; do not let the sun go down on your anger." (Ephesians 4:26) We *can* feel anger and not sin.

I believe it is possible for families, schools, and churches to teach kids moral principles and at the same time to respect the individual, no matter what his behavior. For example, can't we all understand the difference between just *being* bad on the one hand and being good and *doing* something bad on the other? Of course we can. You are not bad just because—if you're like the rest of us—you've done some bad things. This is a big, important difference.

Friends and Close Friends

We must travel in the direction of our fear.

—JOHN BERRYMAN, AMERICAN POET

Another damaging result of our limited way with feelings is that we often find it difficult to have close friends. The women in our lives—girlfriends, wives, partners, relatives, and other friends—often look at us with wonder.

"My son has no friends at all," says one woman I know. "He seems to have acquaintances at work, but no real friends. The thing is, his father has no friends either. I am my husband's only friend." She also expresses her sadness for her son and husband, as well as the pressure she feels to fill all her husband's friendship needs.

But you know what? This tendency to isolation, to be a loner, is something many of us feel from time to time. In fact, we often go back and forth between wanting very much to be part of the crowd and wanting the crowd to stay far away. The goal is to avoid isolation as an ongoing state.

Listen to Edwin A. Robinson's ideas on the friendship of men in these lines from his poem, "Captain Craig," written in 1921:

> —Ah friends, friends,
> There are these things we do not like to know:
> They trouble us, they make us hesitate,
> They touch us and we try to put them off.
> We banish one another and then say
> That we are left alone: the midnight leaf
> That rattles where it hangs above the snow—
> Gaunt, fluttering, forlorn—scarcely may seem
> So cold in all its palsied loneliness

As we, we frozen brothers, who have yet
Profoundly and severely to find out
That there is more of unpermitted love
In most men's reticence than most men think.

"We banish one another and then say that we are left alone."
Ring a bell for you like it did for me when I first read it at the age
of twenty-two? Not that I did much about it then, but at least I
knew something was missing. When twenty years later I grew
tired of being one of a million "frozen brothers," I looked up
Robinson's words again and finally began to do something
about them.

Of course, most of us do have friends. What too many of
us don't have are close friends, "close" meaning one with whom
I am able to be myself completely—vulnerabilities as well as
strengths, seriousness as well as humor, caring as well as dis-
agreeing, anger as well as joy. What keeps us from achieving
this kind of friendship? Is it not the fear I mentioned above?
Somehow this kind of intimacy with another guy is weak and
suspect.

"The problem with our Western culture," writes Edward
Sellner in a 1998 *Common Boundary* article, "is that a man's
desire for . . . communion with other males is the source of
much suspicion. While other societies acknowledge this need,
[much of] Western culture . . . is fearful if not outright con-
demnatory of it." It is, as the poet Robinson says, "unpermitted
love." It often embarrasses us. If this is so, what led us to this
illogical and uncomfortable place?

Again, fear. And we came by it logically. Many of us can recall experiences of shame beginning in childhood and continuing perhaps even to today, experiences that taught us to fear and avoid the expression of care toward another male.

Exhausting Vigilance

If I hazard a guess as to the most endemic, prevalent anxiety among human beings—including the fear of death, abandonment, loneliness—nothing is more prevalent than the fear of one another.

—R. D. Laing, 1927–1989, Scottish psychiatrist

In this exact regard, there is an area of some trouble for many men. This is another place where guts comes into the picture. Please don't skip over this part thinking it doesn't apply to you. The attitude I describe here does a great deal of deep damage to straight men.

Some heterosexual men (as well as some closeted gay men) expend a huge amount of energy on an exhausting vigilance, making absolutely sure that at any given moment the world knows they are *not* gay. It takes a tremendous amount of effort and energy to keep up this vigilance, and it is often kept up at the expense of what they truly enjoy. It is so subtle and pervasive that the individual is frequently unaware of it, so it is not recognized for the serious damage it does. It is a deeply ingrained cultural attitude that has been around for a long time.

This attitude is sometimes called "homophobia," fear of gay people. But I don't think it is an accurate word in this case. I believe the vast majority of straight men are not really afraid of gay men as such. Better would be "effemiphobia" (my word), a fear of the feminine and the effeminate. Because gay men are free to embody both the masculine *and* the feminine, they are often seen as people to be avoided or hurt, based on the fears that association "contaminates," and "weakness" is contagious.

These fears, says psychiatrist and writer Terry Kupers in his excellent book, *Revisioning Men's Lives: Gender, Intimacy, and Power,* are "an important part of male psychology, even in men who would never knowingly support any kind of overt discrimination against gay people."

Thus, what I said earlier about men's attitudes toward feminism can also apply to men's attitudes toward homosexuality. To mock the principles of gay liberation and equality—no matter what your inherited attitude or opinion—is to buy directly into the conspiracy that keeps men half alive.

The oppressor is hurt as much as the oppressed, simply because the burdens of distance, judgment, and fear are exhaustingly impossible to carry. This is an oppression that produces no good.

The literal—although not the most common—meaning of the word *homophobia* is simply "fear of what is the same as you" (*homo* is Greek for "same"). This gets to another hidden but real factor among us: We often are afraid of each other. The historical ideal of the "great love of comrades" has yet to take its place among us.

The good news is that this trend is showing signs of changing. Confident and clear straight men do not fear gay (or bisexual or transgendered) men, just as they do not fear feminism. In fact, they often appreciate and enjoy them. I look forward to the day when all men can approach each other with welcome, with openness, with support, and with friendship. We'll have a different world then.

The man *on* the moon, the astronaut exploring the territory, will at first be cautious of anything or anyone who appears threatening. The man *in* the moon will balance that caution and find ways to celebrate with whomever he finds himself, confident in his own being, open to the other's.

Both are necessary.

If this chapter on damages and differences has led us into the heavier areas of our lives, the next one will lead us to the light again. Because there are preventions for and responses to buried feelings, and to fears, and they are available, right now, to you.

A Few Suggestions for Review

- What feelings do you tend to bury? Fear? Anger? Happiness? Write your answers on a piece of paper; carry it in your pocket. Take it out and look at it occasionally as a reminder not to bury those feelings.
- Look again at a question posed in this chapter: "Do I really believe that buried feelings, can cause serious illness or even death?" You might ask a friend the same question and see what kind of discussion follows.
- Homophobia or "Effemiphobia"? Do you see the difference? Does either have a manifestation in your life or in the lives of your family and friends?
- Look back into the family in which you grew up to see if the answers to the following two questions will bring you insight:

1. When I was a child, how did my father deal with his feelings? Did he bury them? Did he vent them in a rage?
2. Were there times when shame made me bury a feeling very deeply? Take a moment to think back.

four

Three Steps to Emotional Fitness

Now the rubber meets the road. What do you actually do with feelings? How do you deal with them? What are the practical steps for a man to take? The answer is the Three Steps to Emotional Fitness. They are:

- First: Notice the feeling. Stay with it.
- Second: Name the feeling. Pick a name to identify what you feel.
- Third: Express the feeling. Get the feeling outside you.

A Practice for Life

I want to emphasize at the outset that human emotion, its origin and its expression, are very complex and the Three Steps to Emotional Fitness are not intended to be magic bullets. They are not a simplistic answer to a complex question. They really are not an answer at all; they are a practice, a practice for life, a process for health, an exercise for emotional fitness. They can begin to open the way, grease the rails, and establish the habit of a healthy feeling life. The three steps can give you an immense advantage on your road to integrating your astronaut with your man in the moon. Let's look at each of these steps in some detail.

First Step: Notice the Feeling

This first step can seem too easy, almost self-evident, and quite unimportant.

But too often we skip it without knowing that we're skipping something. We just don't notice that we're having feelings. We avoid or ignore them or convince ourselves we don't feel anything. We simply do not notice.

Manual is a forty-two-year-old divorced airline pilot who was in a custody conflict with his ex-wife. When he lost the case and his two children went to live with their mother in a distant city, he said he felt "nothing," that "everything is OK, they're probably better off with her." But he quickly slipped into a deep depression.

He did not notice what he was feeling and so practically ruined his chances of dealing with this difficult situation in a successful way. This not noticing, while understandable because the feelings he avoided are no fun, is just plain disastrous.

Paul, a widower and a retired teacher, suddenly became sad and withdrawn. His friends and family were concerned. "What's going on?" they asked. "Nothing, I'm fine," he'd reply. Then an observant neighbor and friend realized that when he retired from teaching, he lost the most meaningful part of his life. "What do I have to live for now?" he asked her. He did not notice his feeling of depression. He only noticed the pain. His friend did notice it, and she helped him face it, understand it, and move through it. Only then could he move on with his life and not slip into that dark and dangerous place of isolation.

So: when a feeling comes to you, just feel it That's it—just feel it. You don't have to do anything more. But there are some really important things *not* to do. You'll recognize them from chapter 1.

Don't Run

Running from a feeling is often done by distracting yourself, with work or television, for example, or with any one of a million things that need to be done, that need your attention and are often worthy things to do. Running from a feeling can happen so fast—instantaneously and automatically—that the runner has no idea that he is running. This kind of response is often a deeply engrained habit.

Running from a feeling can take many forms. You can physically move away from the situation. Remember Steve, the guy in my office? He walked out of the session and ran from the emotional situation.

You can refuse to talk about a subject; you can avoid, confuse, and bully. You can get sick or have an accident. Or you can suddenly remember a phone call you have to make, a friend you have to visit, or an errand you forgot. Yes, really, none of this is an exaggeration. You can do *anything at all* to avoid noticing the feeling.

The Vietnamese monk and teacher Thich Nhat Hanh has a teaching story about running from the feeling of anger: If your house is on fire, you don't begin to deal with it by chasing after the person you believe started the fire, because your house will burn down. First you put out the fire; then you seek out the arsonist. The same with a feeling. First you must deal with the immediate situation, the fire in front of you: the feeling. Then you can move on to what comes next.

Don't Cover

Covering a feeling is similar to running but not quite as effective. It's easier to spot. A common cover for many men, young and old, is joking or other forms of humor. The joker is almost stereotypical; we all know guys like this. He sees almost everything from a humorous point of view. He just can't seem to get serious, to tell you what's really going on for him. It's always a joke. Now a sense of humor is one of the really likeable traits of people; it's what makes us fun, life funny, and other people enjoyable. But there is a time to be serious.

Other forms of covering are changing the subject, shifting the blame, denying the problem, pretending not to hear, blaring the radio, getting something to eat or drink. Sure, all of these things can be normal parts of life too.

The Feelings of Others

The important thing is being capable of emotions, but to experience only *one's own* would be a sorry limitation.

—ANDRE GIDE, 1869–1951
FRENCH CRITIC AND WRITER

It is not only our own feelings we run from or cover. We often do the same with other people's intense feelings. This is especially true for those raised in families that rarely showed strong feelings, and when they did, they were negative, like criticism and rage.

I recall an incident during a meeting I was attending. A woman became indignant and vocal, to the point of bawling and gesticulating. The soft-spoken man sitting beside me simply got up and walked out, never to return. Too much emotional energy; it signaled danger to him.

Running from or covering other people's feelings can often happen to men when strongly expressed feelings come from women. Their tears, their anger, their powerful and exact words can paralyze us or cause the "flooding" that I mentioned in chapter 2, the overwhelmed feeling.

The key idea in the first step, whether it involves yours or others' feelings, is "notice." That's what we have to do with them, just notice and accept them, experience them, just let them be. Often our first reaction to other's people's feelings, especially strong ones, especially from women, is to do something that will shorten, solve, or end them.

I recall a female client who came to her therapy session angry at her husband. Several days earlier she had a scary car accident that totaled the car. When she came home, shaken but uninjured, and told her husband about it, his first response was, "Don't be upset. It's OK, don't feel bad; we'll get a new car."

From his point of view, it was a kind and supportive response; from hers, it was insensitive and unfeeling. He had done what men tend to do first in response to feelings—offered some helpful thoughts and solutions. But he skipped over her feelings of fear and upset.

"Oh, It's You"

So don't run away from and don't cover either your own or someone else's feelings.

Just take a few deep breaths and feel whatever you're feeling. Let it come, let it be there.

Notice it. Be aware of it. The first step says "Oh, it's you" to the feeling. It is an acknowledgment, a recognition that something new is there, something that wasn't there a minute ago. At first you might not know what the feeling is, what to call it. That makes no difference at this point. What is important is that you know *something is going on in you.*

If at times you realize that you have run from a feeling or have covered it, don't worry. Go back to the feeling again. It will probably still be "there."

The amount of time you spend with the feeling does not

have to be extremely long; a few moments are often enough. You'll find other feelings are with you for hours, weeks, years, or a lifetime.

It might also be true that at any given moment you may not be feeling anything very strongly and thus the noticing step might seem frustrating. While it is understandable for any of us to say *I'm not feeling anything very strongly right now,* this can often be a subtle form of running or covering. So don't let yourself get away with this too much. In any case, it is a good exercise to search for the hint of feeling, the emotional smoke, so to speak.

It is important to make this first step a conscious step, because you can often miss it. You cover the feeling so quickly or run so immediately, that the feeling never has a chance. That's why so many of us can sincerely say *I don't know what I'm feeling.*

This three-step theory is built, in part, on the idea that the feeling "knows" what's best for it—and for you. The feeling can help you know just what to do with it. But it can only do this if it is allowed to stay around for a while to build a relationship with you, its owner. Your emotional well-being depends upon the successful completion of this first step.

It Often Begins in the Body

Your emotions affect every cell in your body. Mind and body, mental and physical, are intertwined.

—THOMAS TUTKO, SPORTS PSYCHOLOGIST

Often, especially with young men, the first sign of the presence of a feeling is some kind of change in your body. Your stomach tightens or aches; the muscles in your arms constrict; your head throbs; your face flushes and your heart races; your hands or feet start shaking. Or, with pleasant feelings, your body relaxes and breathes easily, or you experience a calmness or comfort in your muscles or stomach. Noticing your bodily changes is a good way to start to notice your emotional changes. Almost always, a change in one means a change in the other.

Here is an experience from my own life. When I was graduate student, my most difficult challenge was my relationship with an important professor in my program. I was barely able to contain my dislike when we were together, which was often because this professor kept a tight rein. It was a serious problem; I could not avoid regular contact, and my degree depended on success in his courses.

Whenever I was with my professor my stomach began to tighten, and in a short time I experienced a dull, heavy pain in my gut.

Now, were I able to put the three steps into practice—which I was not at that point—I would have noticed my body, my physical symptoms. The symptoms were obvious: a tightening of the stomach followed by pain. That would have been the first step: *I notice my stomach is reacting to my feelings. The feelings are there and they are strong.* Then I would have been emotionally intelligent. Then I would have been on solid ground in my emotional process because I would have captured, that is, noticed, everything I needed to complete the process with success. Without this first step, all else is doomed.

It's significant to note that even now, as I am writing this at my computer and recalling these incidents from years ago, I still get a vestige of the feeling in my stomach—after all these years. The body also remembers.

So when you notice something going on in your body, ask yourself *What is the flushed and hot feeling in my face and my racing heart trying to tell me?* Or *What feeling is making my palms sweat or my leg twitch?* Or *I have rarely felt so calm and relaxed before; what's going on?* These questions will lead you to identify the feeling you are experiencing—for example, *foolish, sympathetic, embarrassed, peaceful,* or *relaxed.*

Stillpoints

A good way to develop your capacity to notice your feelings is by building the habit of Stillpoints, which I have written about in my book *Stopping: How to Be Still When You Have to Keep Going.* These are easy ways to bring moments of awareness into your day. A Stillpoint is doing nothing, on purpose, to calm down, slow down, and notice what is going on in you.

This noticing, this Stillpoint, is like asking yourself, *What am I feeling right now?* It's the place you have to start; that's why it is the first step. At any given moment in time, in whatever circumstances, you can ask yourself that question. *What's going on in me? What am I feeling right now?*

Stillpoints: Doing Nothing on Purpose to Become Aware of What You're Feeling

This short exercise is very easy, but please don't under-estimate its power. Here's how to do it:

1. Stop what you're doing.
2. Take a deep breath.
3. Close your eyes (if you want) for a moment.
4. Take note of—notice—yourself by turning your focus in.
5. Spend a few moments just being aware of yourself, just here, just now, and what you're feeling. Nothing more. Don't complicate it. It's very simple.

Second Step: Name the Feeling

It is only when we can identify them that we can have some choice about whether to express . . . emotions or not.

—D. BRADFORD AND M. HUCKABAY,
STANFORD BUSINESS SCHOOL

Now that you and the feeling have had some time together, you can move on to the second step, which is to name the feeling. In this step you call the feeling by whatever name seems most accurate. If you want, turn to the list of feelings on pages 36–37 for some of the names you might use.

You can do this naming quietly in your mind or aloud, but be sure to use a specific name. Call it anything, but call it something! You might think, for example, *OK, I'm feeling cheated right now* or *What I'm feeling is overwhelmed* or *This makes me feel uncomfortable.*

Even if you are not sure exactly what the feeling is, name it anyway. Even if it is just the tag end of a feeling that you think you might be having, name it. The very process of naming it will help you know if the name is accurate. *I feel good. I'm feeling happy right now.* This might lead you to *Actually what I'm feeling is satisfied and proud.* You gradually zero in on specific feelings.

This step is important because naming the feeling gives you power over it. Just as when you give a name to your child, or when your parents named you, the naming is a symbol for the position of power and responsibility you have over whom you name.

So it is with feelings. With the second step, you now have established a relationship with a part of yourself and thus have grown in self-knowledge. Now you have some power. Now you don't have to just guess what you're feeling, you know.

You accept ownership of the feeling by naming it. You say, *This is my feeling.* Naming is the acceptance of the reality of the feeling (even though you might not like it) and your ownership of the emotional state (this is my feeling, not yours, nor his, nor hers.) There's no other just like it. Feelings might share names, but, like their owners, they are unique.

To go back to my experience as a graduate student with my professor, when I was noticing the tightening and pain in my stomach, I could have said to myself *What exactly am I feeling? Is it anger? Well, yes. But it's . . . it's that I resent his attitude. He's arrogant as hell! Yes, that's it; he puts everybody down. I resent it!* In other words, I could have put the second step into practice. Those simple acts of first noticing the changes in my body, tightening and pain, and then naming the feelings, anger and resentment, could have put me immediately in a position of power rather than in a position of weakness. Then I would have known and identified—named—what was going on in me. What actually happened was a lot more messy, a result that I now see as avoidable.

Again, please note the shift in power that the second step gives you. By giving the feeling a name, you have shifted the power from the feeling to the feeler, to the part of you that has the capacity to choose what to do about the feeling. Until you do this, the hidden emotion is like a guerilla soldier hiding in ambush, and it has the guerilla's advantage: it sees you, but you don't see it, so it can have its way with you. This step turns the tables.

The names of feelings used in the above examples are: cheated, overwhelmed, uncomfortable, good, happy, satisfied, proud, foolish, sympathetic, embarrassed, anxious, scared, angry, and resentful.

Frustration/Confusion

There's a specific feeling I want to name here. It's really a combination of two feelings, and I believe it is common for men on both extremes of the age spectrum, for men who are new to this

whole emotional process and for men from emotionally dysfunctional families. I call the feeling frustration/confusion.

It's the feeling that comes from not being clear on what to do,
how to act, or what to say, because you don't have enough information to make the right choice. It's the feeling of always having
to guess at what is the right reaction to a situation, when everyone else just naturally seems to know what to do.

This special kind of frustration can often lead to trouble—
exactly because it indicates on the one hand a lack of information and on the other a need to act. A formula for disaster. Here
are a couple of examples.

■ Art and Greg ■

Art was feeling really good, and it was mostly because he just had
a great conversation with a fellow worker, a woman he was interested in dating but did not know very well. They spent several
hours at lunch talking about things they both like. It was a real
high for him, since he had never really talked to her that deeply
before. The next day at work he sees this same co-worker, and as
he approaches her smiling, she gives him a scathing look, turns,
and walks off in the other direction.

And he is left there bleeding. Confusion! Frustration! Of
course he is confused and frustrated. Anyone would be. He has
no explanation for what happened and he doesn't know what
to do. So he throws up his hands and mutters something about
the unpredictability of women.

Greg, a forty-eight-year-old mechanic, is from a very dysfunctional family. Both of his parents were alcoholics, and he suffered a lot of neglect as a child and teenager. He came to counseling specifically about his almost constant feeling of not knowing what everyone else knows. "I'm always just guessing about what to say, what to do, how to act. Everyone else just seems to know it all. How do they know all that? I ask myself. I never really am sure about what I should say to people in a conversation or when I'm asked to express my opinion on something. So I just wing it, take a wild guess and hope for the best. Sometimes it comes out OK, sometimes it doesn't. But I don't know *why* it does or doesn't! Am I crazy?"

No, Greg is not crazy. There's a reason he always has to guess and has no confidence about what to say or do: He was never taught, either through modeling or specific teaching. Frustration and confusion are his constant companions.

Art, as he noticed and named his normal feelings about the situation with the woman at work, gained enough confidence in what he was feeling to follow it up. He asked her about it. It turned out to be a misunderstanding based on office gossip. And Greg, once assured that his responses were understandable, given his history, decided this process of managing his feelings was not only valuable, but doable.

So what I am suggesting to Art and Greg is—that's right—the first two steps: Stay with the frustration for a while, just feel it. Don't run, don't cover! Then call it a name: *You are that $%^&* frustration (or hurt or confusion)!*

Can you see how these two steps give these guys power and more control over what they're feeling? With these two steps they are also giving themselves more time. And time is always a necessary ingredient to resolve confusion and frustration.

Modifying the Name

McKay, Fanning, and Paleg in their book, *Couple Skills,* have devised a way of refining the naming process of the second step.

Once you have the name for the feeling, you can modify it. That is, you can refine it and zero in on what exactly the feeling is by finding modifiers. Here are their suggested ways to modify, and thus clarify, the name of the feeling (in italics) that you have chosen:

- Define it: "My *sadness* is a deep and isolating sadness."
- Rate its intensity: "The *rage* I feel is so strong it scares me."
- Tell its duration: "I have felt this *jealousy* since the day we met."
- Give a context: "I'm *annoyed* because cleaning this mess takes time from my work."
- Give a historical perspective: "My *fear* takes me back to my childhood fear of being left out, of never being chosen."

The reason for this modifying process is to achieve more accuracy, to give the name(s) you have chosen for your feeling(s) even more precision and clarity.

So now you have the first two steps in place: You noticed the presence of a feeling that exists in you because you have not run, you have not covered. You stayed with it and looked at it, that is, at yourself and at what you are feeling at the moment. Then you have given that emotional state a name—sad, mad, glad, frustrated—and thus changed the balance of power in your favor.

Third Step: Express the Feeling

If you bring forth what is within you, what you bring forth will save you. If you do not bring forth what is in you, what you do not bring forth will destroy you.

—JESUS, GOSPEL OF THOMAS

Now—and *only* now, after the first two steps—are you ready to move on. Only now are you in a position to play the whole game of life and not just half of it. Only now do you welcome both the logical, thinking moments and the spontaneous, feeling moments. You are the astronaut walking on the moon, ready to jump, to take a wild, abandoned leap into the world of the man in the moon. No longer dominated by cautions, fears, or hesitations, your leap becomes a transformation.

The third step is, of course, the next logical step: expressing the feeling. By "express" I mean externalize, which means to get the feeling out of the internal world of yourself and into the external world of everyone else. Give the feeling outward expression. Tell it in some way to some part of the world. Get what's inside outside.

■ Ben's Dance ■

Years ago when I was teaching junior English in high school, I had a student, Ben. He was generally a good student, but he always had a hard time with writing. One particular writing assignment, something on your favorite subject, really got his interest because his favorite subject was the Basque culture group he belonged to. He was determined to write the best essay he ever wrote. And he did. It was an excellent piece of writing, well organized, with correct grammar, full of his enthusiasm and appreciation of his Basque heritage, and it kept your interest for all five pages. I gave the grade I thought it deserved: A+, the first Ben had ever received on a writing assignment.

After all these years, I can still picture it. Right after the class in which he received his paper back, Benny was doing what I can only describe as a wild and crazy dance down the hallway. Arms and legs flying in every direction, head bopping up and down, now jumping, now running, hands waving and circling. Everyone just stopped and stared. *What in the world is going on with Benny?*

In our terms, Ben was doing the third step. He was getting out the feelings that were inside him—happiness, success, fulfillment, and satisfaction—and doing it in a spontaneous and memorable way.

Going Public

Up to this point in our process, you could have done steps one and
two in a crowd and no one would have necessarily known that
you were up to something. With this step, you go public. It can
be public in a small, quiet way that draws no attention at all. Or
it can be public in a big, noisy way that draws a lot of attention.
The third step is also a step into the realm of morality, as mentioned in chapter 2. With the externalization of your feelings, you
are responsible and accountable.

Examples of the successful externalization of feelings cover
the spectrum from the petty and pitiful to the magnificent and
mystical. It can be the snapping of your fingers in the feeling of
frustration or the writing of a song from a feeling of passion.
You can wail your agony or yell your enthusiasm. You can speak
your concern or you can jump for joy.

You can tell a friend you're excited or mad. You can write
poetry to someone you love, moved by loneliness; or letters to
your senator, moved by anger. You dance for happiness (like
Ben) or sigh from contentment. You defend your country out
of a feeling of patriotism or mow the lawn as an expression of
pride. You demonstrate on the capitol steps as an expression
of a deep conviction.

The expressions are: snapping of fingers, writing a song,
wailing, yelling, speaking, jumping, telling, writing poetry and
letters, dancing, sighing, defending, mowing, and demonstrat-
ing. All are external, discernible acts. Some last a moment;
others may span a lifetime.

Think of almost anything you do—sports, homework, time with family, hanging out with friends, music (listening or playing), giving a present, getting evaluations, writing a report—*anything* can be the expression, the externalization, of a feeling. You can see that the examples are endless, because they include everything we do.

External

Whatever the mode of expression, it must be external to you. The feeling must be moved out, put in the exterior. And that has to be done in some physical, perceptible way. If you were videotaped during this step, you would be seen *doing* or *saying* something, though the meaning of your actions or words might not be evident. In this step, the emotional is given physical expression outside your body.

> **Successful and accomplished people find really good ways to express their feelings. It's a major component of their success.**

Think of the people you admire, perhaps sports or civic leaders (like Tiger Woods or Abraham Lincoln or Lou Gehrig) or those closer to home, maybe a teacher, neighbor, relative, or friend. At least part of the reason you admire them is because they found really good ways to express what they were feeling.

The third step is the part that makes these the steps to emotional *fitness*. Why? Because it allows feelings to do what feelings were meant to do. Psychologist James Pennebaker puts it bluntly: "If you don't talk out your traumas, you're screwed. I think that's the scientific term for it." "Pennebaker has shown," reports a March 16, 1998 *Newsweek* article, "that when people regularly talk or even write about things that are upsetting to them, their immune systems perk up and they require less medical care." The talking or writing is the third step. It externalizes the feeling.

Meeting the Conditions

The challenge here is to express the feeling in ways that meet certain conditions. These conditions are somewhat obvious, but I believe they're worth mentioning for clarity:

- The first condition is that the expression you choose must do its main task: express your feeling for you. That's basic. If that doesn't work, forget it. If you want to express your overwhelming appreciation for something your sister did for you, then probably a casual "Thanks, Sis" over your shoulder as you go out the door is not going to get the job done (for you, never mind for her).

- Secondly, to be a successful expression, it must not violate your personal value system; that is, it must not damage you or anyone else and it must be in agreement with your own code of ethics. If you express your frustration all the time by screaming at your spouse, it's not going to turn out so good.

Do you see that the three steps are life itself? That's what I mean when I said in chapter 2 that "feeling is everything." All that you do is motivated by feelings, and how those feelings are noticed, named, and expressed is profoundly important because it determines the very quality of your life. In fact, the three steps *are* your life.

You are free to externalize in ways that are noble and honorable or in ways that are dirty and mean. What we see and understand of each other's lives is the way we do our three steps. An autobiography is essentially telling the world how you have lived the three steps: *This is what I felt and this is what I did about it.*

Anger

> The man who gets angry at the right things and with the right people, and in the right way and at the right time and for the right length of time, is commended.
>
> —ARISTOTLE, *NICOMACHEAN ETHICS*

One feeling in particular merits a special note: anger. If this feeling is a problem for you, you're not alone. It seems that modern life is full of poor expressions of male anger. Just listening to the news a few evenings a week proves that.

Traits of Emotionally Healthy People

Ron and Pat Potter-Efron point out in their book *Letting Go of Anger* some of the ways that emotionally healthy people handle anger. The following techniques are based on their ideas. Check them out to see if they make sense to you.

- **They treat anger as a normal part of life.** Everybody gets angry at one time or another. All of us. It's human.

- **They see that anger is an accurate signal of real problems in a person's life.** So anger has its useful purpose. It alerts us to real problems.

- **They screen angry actions carefully; they needn't get angry automatically just because they could.** The key word here is "get." You notice you're feeling angry (first step); you name it as "anger at my boss" (second step); your third step is perhaps to wait a while and then approach your boss with the reason for your anger, rather than to "get angry" right in his face.

- **Anger is expressed in moderation so there's no loss of control.** People who are emotionally healthy are good at picking the right time to do the third step, and the right place, too.

- **Their goal is to solve problems, not just to express anger.** Remember wallowing? If the goal is to resolve whatever challenge presents itself, the temptation to wallow will be weakened. That's good.

- **Their anger is clearly stated in ways others can understand.** Much better to say to your friend, "I am really mad at you for telling what you promised to keep secret," than to avoid him (and hold your anger) for a month.

- **They see that anger is temporary. It can be relinquished once an issue is resolved.** No one is more boring and dull than someone who is "always angry." People learn to stay away.

Dealing with Anger

Here are a few suggestions for practicing the third step, when the feeling is "ANGER!"

- Recognize the signs of anger and make part of your third step a weakening of the energy by conscious breathing, counting to ten slowly, or talking over the situation with someone you trust.

- Practice a relaxation technique like doing a Stillpoint (see page 106) or taking a short walk. Also useful are Asian arts such as yoga, tae kwan do, or tai chi, a series of slow, purposeful movements.

- Identify and, if possible, avoid circumstances that trigger anger. Arrange and plan your life so as to avoid what you know will make you mad. If possible, simply leave a situation that will feed your anger.

- Exercise is often a great way to do the third step if you're feeling angry. Medical specialists tell us that it is also very good for your health.

Postponing and Substituting

> There is perhaps no . . . skill more fundamental than resist-
> ing impulse. It is the root of all emotional control, since all emo-
> tions lead to [an] impulse to act.
>
> —DANIEL GOLEMAN, PSYCHOLOGIST

There are two special circumstances we need to understand about
the third step; both are occasions when it is necessary to *resist*
the impulse to express a feeling. They are when we need to postpone the expression of a feeling or to substitute one expression
of a feeling for another.

To decide not to express a feeling at any given moment, in
other words, to postpone it, is not the same as avoiding it.
Usually, the sooner and the more immediate the expression,
the better. But one can and, at times, should postpone the expression of a feeling. The decision to postpone is, in some way, a
fulfilling of the third step. It's what you're doing with the feeling right now; you're postponing it.

> The greatest remedy for anger is delay.
>
> Seneca, First-century Roman philosopher

You might wisely decide to postpone your feeling of frustration with your business partner until you are feeling calmer
and cooler or until you are in a situation that shows you she is
open to hear your criticism.

You might be feeling great impatience with a youngster and decide to delay the expression of the feeling until both you and the youngster are in a more tension-free situation.

The serious danger with postponement is that you will never return to the feeling to give it more explicit expression, and it slips into a burial vault. Again, always revisit a postponed feeling.

■ Substitution: Ted and Eric ■

Quid pro quo literally means (in Latin) "something for something." Most the time it means you get something back for what you give. I want to use it a little differently. Often you will want to express your feeling indirectly, substituting a symbolic expression for a real one, expressing *this something* in the place of *that something*. *Quid pro quo* is a great way to do the third step and can get you out of many tight fixes. Freud called it sublimation, an effective way to substitute a healthy impulse for an antisocial one.

For example, Ted feels a strong dislike for his sister's husband. He has tried to like him but he just doesn't. He can't help it. That's what he feels. Having identified and named the feeling (dislike for my brother-in-law), Ted decides not to express this feeling directly to anyone in his family. This could well be a mature and wise decision.

But to keep healthy in his process of feelings, he must express it; that is, he has to do the third step. So he finds a substitute way or a symbolic way to do the expression; he finds a *quo* for his *quid.* In this case, Ted decides to write extensively and honestly about his negative feeling in his journal. He might also have waited until he was out jogging alone and could scream his feelings to the sky, or he could have directed his negative feelings into his workout at the gym. He substitutes expressing the feeling to his journal (or to the sky or into physical exercise) for expressing the feeling to his family. But here's the important thing: the feeling still gets expressed.

Here's another common situation in which to do the third step by substitution. Eric has a job at a high-tech firm. It's a great job, with decent money and a flexible schedule. He desperately needs the job because his wife is expecting their third child. The problem is his new department manager. He's a small-minded man and not too bright. He constantly chides Eric, makes fun of his clothes, lies about the amount of time he's worked, and generally makes life miserable. He's also the CEO's second cousin.

This is a damned-if-you-do/damned-if-you-don't situation. If he complains to his manager's boss, it will just make things worse. If he quits his job, well, he *can't* quit his job. He needs it too badly. He has tried repeatedly without success to talk directly to his manager.

What can Eric do? He has completed the first two steps: he knows the feelings that he's been having for several months; he has named them clearly: frustration and anger. Now what?

What Eric did was this: Since he and his brother (who worked at the same company) were very close, he told his brother exactly what he was feeling. He knew his brother would give him a sympathetic hearing, which he did. Eric was also active in a discussion group and was used to talking about problems with the group. So, in confidence he told the group about the situation and what he was feeling. They responded with interest and with some practical suggestions.

These substitutions made work bearable. Instead of expressing his feelings to his boss, Eric substituted expressing his feelings to his brother and receiving his empathy, and talking to his group and getting suggestions. In fact, his change in attitude seemed to soften the effects his manager had on him. There are other ways Eric could have done this substitution, like directing his aggressive feelings toward a tennis ball.

But keep in mind the risk of postponing the expression of feelings and substituting ways of expressing them directly: burial. If you postpone, get back to it! If you substitute, do it as soon as possible!

The Quick Three-Step

Use this quick version of the Three Steps to Emotional Fitness anytime—while you're in the car, during a class break, at your computer, as you walk down the street, as you wait in line, on your way home, anytime. Just remember: Notice, Name, Express.

1. Notice: Ask yourself *What am I feeling right now?* Stay with the question a few moments if the answer doesn't come right away. This is when it is important not to give up. Be patient with yourself. Let the feeling be present to you slowly.

2. Name: Use a word or words to name the feeling(s) you have. If you are alone, say the name(s) out loud: *I'm nervous about the exam. I'm anxious about it. Nervous and anxious.* If you're with someone else, you can keep your names internal. (Why not combine steps 2 and 3 and tell the person you're with what you're feeling? *I'm really nervous about this exam.*)

3. Express: How can you externalize the feeling(s) right now? Use your imagination. Tell someone what you're feeling. Find some "anxious" music on the radio, make and unmake a fist, sing, yell, write, sigh, smile. Do you see? It really makes no difference what you do! *Do something*—anything!—to express the feeling.

Telling It

"Tell us thy troubles and speak freely. A flow of words doth ever ease the heart of sorrows; it is like opening the waste where the mill dam is overfull."

—HOWARD PYLE

ROBIN HOOD, *THE MERRY ADVENTURES OF ROBIN HOOD*

Perhaps the most common and the most helpful use of *quid pro quo* is simply telling someone you trust what's going on with you. Take the feeling that you're having and, instead of expressing it directly to the person or at the situation, tell someone else, someone you trust. For example:

- You don't want to tell your ill father you're disappointed with something he did, but you can tell a trusted friend.
- It seems wrong to keep complaining about your sister-in-law's annoying friends, but your buddy will understand how you feel.
- You have a very embarrassing feeling about someone so you decide to trust it only to your pastor.
- Your neighbor is in serious trouble and you are feeling uncomfortable about it, so you decide to confide in an older friend.

The examples could go on forever. So remember: If you have a hard time finding a good way to do the third step, look for some trusted person and *simply tell them what you're feeling.*

I know this works. Remember? I am a family counselor, and one way to understand what happens in counseling is to see it as the third step. People just like you and me come in to my office and tell me what they are feeling. Telling someone else what has happened in your life—your stories and your feelings about them—means that now someone else carries them with you, you carry less of the weight, so to speak. It works. I couldn't tell you how many times a client has said something like "Just talking about it makes me feel better."

Why the Three Steps Work

These steps do work; there is no doubt about that. The three steps are effective because they are based on the actual ways feelings operate. They are nothing more than doing what comes naturally. What is described in these steps is just what people naturally do; people, that is, who have not been shortchanged in their training about emotional health.

By following these steps, your feelings will do what they were born to do: put you in contact with life by getting expressed in an acceptable way. They will not become buried alive and then attack you in the form of addictive behavior, serious illness, or striking out at someone else physically or verbally.

The very word *emotion* helps us here. It is from two Latin roots: *e* means "out" and *movere* means "to move." An emotion is born precisely in order to move out.

But beyond the satisfaction of being able to "move it out," the three steps will lead you to live a *whole* life, a life built on a balance between thinking and feeling.

In the give-and-take of everyday living, the steps are not always so clearly separated, one from the other, as they are on these pages. As you are in the process of step one, you might also be beginning step three, and then move to step two. They overlap and intertwine. But they are always three distinct processes: noticing, naming, and expressing, and in most situations they stay pretty much in order.

A Few Suggestions for Review

- Sometime soon make a couple photocopies of The Quick Three-Step exercise on page 124: Keep one handy, maybe in your wallet, for easy reference.
- Try to think of a time when you ran from or covered a feeling. What would *not* running or *not* covering have looked like in those situations?
- Try to do the Quick Three-Step three times a day, until you get used to it and it becomes a natural part of your life.
- Quickly review the Quick Three-Step.

five

Care and Feeding of the Three Steps

This final chapter has to do with creating favorable environments in which to practice your new skills with feelings, to put in place as many supports as possible to assure a successful outcome; in other words, the care and feeding of the Three Steps to Emotional Fitness. Don't underestimate the effect of putting these steps into practice. It might make some big differences in your life. Watch for signs from other people that tell you they are noticing something different—comments, looks, or other indications that they've noticed. Let's begin with the idea of reinvention.

Reinventing Yourself

It's one of the most valuable skills of contemporary life, used alike by politicians and rock stars: the ability to reinvent yourself. Gone are the days when it was common to have one job and live in the same place your whole lifetime. Reinvention is now a permanent part of life because change is constant and pervasive. Often it also is unannounced: a new job, a new family, a different place to live, changed priorities, getting or loosing money, an illness (yours or someone else's), new opportunities undreamed of before—or a new way of dealing with your feelings. All of these situations call for a new you. By following the path of this book you are making changes not only in your life, but in the way others will see you, and that constitutes a kind of reinvention, a new part of you coming to life.

Following are some ideas to keep in mind in this process of self-reinvention. Please don't see them as "things I gotta do" but rather, as you read through them, see which ones you already do, which ones to keep in mind for the future, and maybe one area you want to start on soon. The ideas come under the headings: Communication, Getting Together with Friends, Imagination, Spirituality, Exercise, Hunting (yes, hunting; you'll see), and Children.

Communication

If you would have me weep, you must first of all feel grief yourself.

—HORACE, POET, 65–8 B.C.E.

The realization that the Three Steps to Emotional Fitness are in fact a self-reinvention might first become evident in your processes of communication, especially with a spouse, significant other, or close friend. Those who are closest to you are likely to notice the changes you are making and might not know how to respond.

This is normal; they have to get used to the reinvented you. It's likely also that you will make some missteps as you journey along. This too is to be expected. Your feelings might have, for example, a high degree of defensiveness: *This is what I feel and I don't care what you say about it!* Such an attitude might be overwhelming to the other person, who in turn doesn't have a clue how to respond.

One of the ways you might help communication is by making a concentrated effort to use "I" statements. It is a chief characteristic of all good communication, especially when it involves feelings. Use "I" statements rather than "You" statements. That means telling what is going on for you rather than saying what you think is going on for someone else. In doing so, you avoid blaming, which, even if you think the other person *is* to blame, kills communication. Compare these pairs of statements:

"You're always late, so we never arrive anywhere on time. It drives me crazy!" ("You" statement. Implication: it's your fault.)

"I am very frustrated when we arrive late. I feel rude and inconsiderate." ("I" statement. Implication: I have a problem.)

"All your time and energy is on the kids. The rest of the world just has to take care of itself, I guess." ("You" statement, blaming.)

"I have been feeling left out of your life recently." ("I" statement.)

"I" statements are a staple commodity in the life of any effective conversation. They will always put you in a better position to bring the communication to a satisfying conclusion—especially as you're experimenting with the three steps.

Getting Together with Friends

Lack of social connection is "the largest unexplored issue in men's health."

—*MEN'S HEALTH* MAGAZINE, OCT. 2001

If there is only one change that you make as a result of reading this book, please make it this one. *Please!* Determine somehow, some way, at some time to regularly get together with friends; that is, if you don't already do it. This simple decision may look innocent and common, but it is a profound investment in mental and emotional health.

This getting together can take many forms. Find one (or more) that is just right for you. Here are some examples:

- Sports: Have a regular time and place to meet your buddy—or several—for a game of racquetball, golf, bicycling, or whatever your game is.
- Food: Meet with a group of friends for a regular meal at one of your homes or a restaurant.
- Group: Join or start some kind of group that meets regularly: book group, support group, investment group, hobby group, etc.

- Poker: Gather a group of guys who love poker or any other game and meet on a regular basis to play.
- Church: Join a group in your church that meets regularly around some topic of interest to you.
- Clubs: The many service clubs (Kiwanis, Rotary, Toastmasters, etc.) or other kinds of clubs offer opportunities to get together regularly with other members to work on some project or service.

Did you notice the word that is in every example? *Regular.* The emphasis is on regular connecting, rather than on habitual isolation. The movement is away from feeling competitive with other guys toward feeling connected with them socially. And this isn't just fun, statistics prove it's healthy.

In his book *Bowling Alone,* Harvard professor Robert Putnam describes the importance of social connection for men: "As a rough rule of thumb, if you belong to no groups but decide to join one, you cut your risk of dying over the next year in half."

Isolation is not healthy. Experience shows, over and over again, that social isolation—not having anyone with whom you can share you life, your thoughts, your cares, your personal feelings—greatly increases the chances of sickness or death. We were not meant to live alone. Social interaction improves health. Getting together does not have to be anything that explores our inner hopes and dreams, although many of us want to do exactly that. Just get together with some friends and do whatever you enjoy: talk, play some games, have a few drinks, and enjoy yourself. It's about connecting, tapping into something greater than yourself.

The best way to find a group is to start one. Several years ago, I realized I was working too much and not attending to all aspects of my life. I took a chance and asked one friend if he wanted to get together and talk about a book that we had both recently read. He said "Sure, why not." We did, and then moved on to read another book and meet over lunch to talk about it.

Soon we asked a third friend to join us. He did. We kept reading books but added what we call a "check-in," when each of us talks a bit about what's been going on with us lately. The three of us asked a fourth and kept meeting about once a month taking turns hosting. We meet from six to nine o'clock in the evening. We talk about all kinds of stuff. Once in a while we go out for drinks and dinner.

Individual members have come and gone, but the group has been going for ten years.

Which factor has the greatest impact on your health—exercise, food, or emotional well-being?

In a survey by the Wirthlin Worldwide polling organization, 60% of Americans picked "emotional well-being."

UC Berkeley
Wellness Letter, Mar. 2001

What Can You Imagine?

Imagination is more important than knowledge.

—ALBERT EINSTEIN

The three steps (Notice, Name, and Express), especially the third, challenge the imagination. This wonderful power, I believe, is the most underused and undervalued of all human faculties, and one which holds enormous untapped potential for men. Our imaginations are untapped for many reasons, not the least of which is their intimate connection with feelings. Feelings and imagination are very close friends; they hang out together.

Samuel Taylor Coleridge, the English poet, called the imagination "the prime agent of all human perception, the human equivalent of the creative power of the universe." Feel the power of those words. You have within you the same "creative power" as that of the entire universe. And, like most of us, you probably use about one-tenth of the power.

Susan Faludi, in her book *Stiffed: The Betrayal of the American Man,* says that in an age when men are searching for authentic ways to express masculinity, they need to keep in mind that their task "is not, in the end, to figure out how to be masculine—rather, [their] masculinity lies in figuring out how to be human." It is imagination more than anything that makes us human.

So, how will you imagine? What tangible forms will your imagination give to your feelings? No one else will be able to express feelings the way you can express yours. This is how your life becomes your life. Repeat: No one else will be able to express feelings the way that *you* express yours. This is how your life becomes *your* life.

What expressions will your feelings of peace take? How will your joy become externalized? What can you imagine to do with your anger? Your resentment? Your hurt? How will the world experience your feelings of lust, zeal, arrogance, greed, generosity, bliss, cheer, enthusiasm? The answers to these questions—and especially to your own personal questions—are not only important, they are your life and what your life will become. And, not incidentally, they will have an effect on all your relationships with others and on all the rest of the world.

What can you imagine? How will you express it? Remember the power. There is no limit. All great men, both the famous and the unknown, have imagined greatly. Their noble deeds and creative expressions of feelings—that is, their third step—were first brought to life in imagination.

Three famous men practice the third step:

"Not to transmit an experience is to betray it."

Elie Wiesel, Nobel prize-winning author

"I wonder how all those who do not write, compose or paint can manage to escape the . . . fear which is inherent in the human situation."

Graham Greene, novelist

"The only way to get rid of my fears is to make films about them."

Alfred Hitchcock, film director

Spirituality

Sensation establishes what is actually given, thinking enables us to recognize its meaning, feelings tell us its value.

—KARL JUNG, SWISS PHYSICIAN AND PSYCHOLOGIST

I want to mention the life of the spirit (spirituality) as a source of emotional life and power, hoping that mentioning it only briefly will not detract from its preeminent importance and value, and realizing that there are many who do not like the words.

The main point I want to make is this: Spirituality is really quite simple. There's no need to make it mysterious and complicated. The life of the spirit can be understood simply as the *meanings and values by which you live your life* and, if you are a believer, *the way you access the divine.* Anything you do to feed, enhance, support, or exercise what is *meaningful and valuable* to you is your spirituality. The process may involve religion or not. With this definition, everyone has spirituality of some kind. Whether or not you are religious makes no difference; long-established as well as recent practices have shown that spirituality can thrive totally outside the boundaries of organized religion.

I said at the beginning of this book that I have neither the power nor any desire to tell you *what* to feel; rather my only goal is to aid in the process of identifying and expressing *whatever* you feel in a healthy way. Well, what you feel and especially how you express it depend on your spirituality, that is, on what you hold meaningful and valuable. So what I am calling spirituality is indeed important. It not only determines what kind of person you are, it determines how the rest of the world experiences you.

Everything we have been discussing is in the spiritual realm. Although they frequently have physical dimensions, feelings are spiritual realities. Systems of spirituality, whether churches or other kinds of spiritual groups, can be powerful sources of life-giving energy and ways to connect with the divine, however you conceive it—God, the supernatural, a higher power, or the universe as a whole.

For many followers of the great spiritual paths, the three steps we've been talking about are achieved on a transcendent plane, and there is no need for the separate steps. They live on a mystical level and in a unitive dimension where steps are blurred by love.

Unfortunately, there are many spiritual counterfeits, not only lurking in the theological back roads of the world, but often sharing center stage on television or the local stadium. Caution, prudence, and a trust in your own common sense are good companions on your journey. Indeed, in trying to discern authentic spiritual groups you have a perfect opportunity to exercise both parts of your new self: the cautious, careful man on the moon, and the spontaneous, enthusiastic man in the moon.

Two additional points in regard to spirituality:

First, one of the great contributions to America's health has been the twelve-step program of Alcoholics Anonymous. The twelve steps are now used worldwide as a spiritually based process to overcome all kinds of addictions and dysfunctional conditions.

Second, deep, diaphragmatic breathing has been connected to spiritual practices for centuries and is still one of the most effective responses to a stressful situation. Focusing on your breathing, learning to breathe deeply, frequently, will always make an emotional challenge more manageable, and an emotional pleasure more enjoyable.

Exercise

I go for two kinds of men. The kind with muscles, and the kind without.

—MAE WEST

Whether they want to build up their muscles or not, many men find physical exercise their prime stress management tool. The statistics are readily available and totally convincing: The benefits of regular exercise are overwhelming. It improves literally everything. It helps deal with stress and it improves health, emotional and physical. This is an aspect of life that many men fully understand and embrace.

So the simple truth is this: Continue regular exercise if you already do it; begin regular exercise if you don't. It is one of the most important investments in a full, healthy, and happy life that you can make.

A personal note: I don't enjoy exercise. I wish I did. My friend Mike loves it. He goes to the gym often and is always saying how much he enjoys the weightlifting, the treadmill, and the stepper. I envy him. But I have found a solution: I walk. I try to do it every day, for two miles, briskly. My next step is to add some weights and aerobics (which is a step—I must be truthful— that I have been *talking* about for several years).

Hunting

I go among trees and sit still.

—WENDELL BERRY, AMERICAN POET

Some of my pleasant memories from boyhood are of the times I went duck hunting on the shores of Lake Erie with my father and older brothers. We stayed in a motel overnight and got up at four in the morning to be out in the blind before dawn. Watching for the ducks, drinking hot chocolate against the freezing weather, seeing the ducks come in and settle on the water, jumping up and trying to pick one out of the flock, and just being part of the whole effort was great fun. But it is the stillness I remember best, the stillness while just sitting and waiting in the dark, cold duck blind.

I still hunt, but my hunting now is for stillness. Let me explain. Still Hunting is a practice I learned from naturalist Joseph Cornell in his book *Listening to Nature.* He learned it from an American Indian tradition. It consists of first finding a quiet place in nature, somewhere you will not be seen or disturbed, a bit hidden, perhaps in a very large park or somewhere in the country, in the mountains or desert. Then just settle down for a while, sitting comfortably, and remain as still as you can. "Just melt into the landscape and let nature come back to life around you." Then just notice what you see, hear, and feel. Just notice. Sit for twenty minutes.

The energy that enlivens the practice of Still Hunting is at the opposite end of the spectrum from spending time with friends. This is time with yourself, and it is very conducive to the first step, noticing. It is a practice that will be more attractive to introverts, like me, than to those of you who are extroverts, to whom this may sound quite mad. I also believe it is a particularly appealing way to find stillness for men.

But whether you practice Still Hunting or not, spending quiet time in nature is the idea here. Try to find some regular way to do that.

The Children! The Children!

What's done to children, they will do to society.

—Karl Menninger, 1893–1990,

American physician

The focus of this work is teenagers and adults, not children, but it seems urgent to me to add a section here about children—specifically boys—because it is in childhood that we first meet the forces that lead us far from our emotional life. I want to speak of only two principles, which, if we were to practice them, could work to avoid what got most of us into trouble. The first principle is this: Children, especially boys, act out what they feel.

That's it: Children act out what they feel. I have relied heavily here on Adele Faber and Elaine Mazlish in their excellent book *How to Talk So Kids Will Listen and Listen So Kids Will Talk.* To relate successfully to children, you *must* know what they are feeling, because that's the only way to know how they are. As children, they do not have well developed thinking skills. But, oh, what feelers they are! That's really almost all they do, feel. Remember the principle: Children *act out* what they feel.

Observing the child's acting out—or behavior—and then identifying the feeling it manifests places you in the right position to first accept then respond to the feeling. Accepting what the child feels is often more difficult than it might sound. But it is urgent to do so. Faber and Mazlish present this conversation. Does it ring true for you?

Child: That TV show was boring.

You: No it wasn't. It was very interesting.

Child: It was stupid.

You: It was educational.

Child: It stunk.

You: Don't talk that way!

Do you see what has happened here? It has become an argument. You could have responded to the child's remark, *which is the feeling acted-out,* by accepting that the child found the TV show boring: "Oh, you found it boring. That's interesting. Tell me why." It's that simple. Now the child feels accepted and will be more willing to hear your opinion. This, of course, is only doing to a child what we all would like when we express feelings.

You are also holding the youngster accountable for what he expresses. After you have done this for a while, the kid will see that what he puts out there will be heard, considered, and taken seriously. Thus he will learn to do a self-check as he expresses a feeling, an important step toward accountability and maturity.

By the way, it isn't only children who act out what they feel. We all do. It's just that we get better at hiding the feelings as we get older and a bit battle scarred. Nevertheless, it's a good principle to keep in mind for adults too.

The second principle is this: Boys need men in their lives.

Since the industrial revolution, boys have been raised primarily by women. Thus, as mentioned in chapter 3, we generally learn feelings from women. When we discover that we are unable to feel in the all the same ways that women feel, parts of us become numb and we have to operate with a wounded feeling function.

Boys have no opportunity to be initiated by older males into the "male mode of feeling"—Poet Robert Bly's apt expression—

DEAR ABBY: I had an eye-opening experience Sunday. Our 13-year-old son has always seemed fairly happy and well adjusted. As we were about to leave for church, I looked at him and I could feel that something was not right. His face had a desperate look. I asked him, "Are you OK?" and that was all it took. My boy began sobbing and told me he'd been crying every night for the past two weeks.

I immediately began asking all kinds of questions. I told him we would get him help the next day. Just the fact that I believed him and was willing to take action seemed to lift some of the burden he's been carrying around.

His father and I and both of his grandparents have all had problems with depression. The doctor later told our son how fortunate he is to have parents who don't minimize their children's feelings. I cannot impress enough to parents the importance of paying attention to their children's moods and body language.

GRATEFUL MOTHER
IN MINNESOTA

(*Dear Abby* column, 10-26-02)

which was common for boys in primitive and even earlier civilized societies.

Author and therapist Michael Gurian takes up the idea in his work *The Good Son:* "If we had to look at the top problem right now in our culture, the lack of fathers and other older males in the lives of young males would have to be at the top."

This lack can lead to serious problems, such as men becoming competitive with women rather than complementary and cooperative; or men being unable to form strong, meaningful, friendships with other men, because of fear. It can help explain the anger that some men in our society hold toward women and toward other men as evidenced in the national statistics on crimes of violence and abuse (wife beating, gay bashing, serial killing). Says Gurian, pulling no punches, "Women are having to bond with half-men, with boys who were not fully raised to manhood, don't know how to bond, don't know what their responsibilities are to humanity, and don't have a strong sense of service. All of those are what manhood is."

Joseph Cornell, in his book *Listening to Nature* quotes biologist Rachel Carson: "If a child is to keep alive his inborn sense of wonder . . . he needs the companionship of at least one adult who can share it." Without the parenting, mentoring, coaching, caring, and just lending a hand on the part of older males, boys are left only half-developed.

Imagine for a moment that all boys were taught emotional fitness by the men in their lives. I believe most violence would disappear. This is another way to understand the emotional literacy that we mentioned in chapter 1.

If you had the intention of teaching emotional literacy to boys, just what would you teach them? By way of an answer, Kindlon and Thompson, in *Raising Cain,* suggest some things

that we can teach boys. They call these the "lessons of emotional literacy" and they include ideas such as:

- Life is not always fair, so you have to learn to deal with
  it as it is.
- You can't go around hurting people every time you're
  angry.
- You need to keep in mind how your behavior might
  affect other people.
- Don't look for threats where there are none.
- Controlling your anger does *not* make you a sissy.

For a moment, examine your own attitudes toward these
lessons that are meant to teach boys. Read them over again to
see if you really agree with them. I mean agree with them not
only with your mind but also with your soul, believe in them
so that you try to live them.

So, the two principles again: (1) Boys act out what they feel.
(2) Boys need older males to care about them and teach them
the lessons of emotional literacy. Perhaps the practicing of these
principles can be a way for you to pass on a legacy of emotional
health and well-being to the next generation.

Cautions, Loose Ends, and Helps

Remember as you become more aware of your feelings, especially if this is a new experience for you, that the first feelings
you become aware of might be negative ones. The experience

could be menacing and make you feel out of control and thus hesitant to continue this process of emotional growth. Try not to confuse the experience of negative feelings, such as fear or grief, with the process of becoming a more feeling person. The experience will pass; the process will endure and serve you well.

Buried feelings can become very strong as a result of being repressed and frustrated over a long time, so it is important to be cautious with them. If your old, buried feelings are anger, resentment, revenge, and such, you could do great harm to someone, either to the person who is the object of those feelings or to some innocent person on whom your feelings get projected.

Likewise, if your long-repressed feelings are self-hate and depression, you could be a danger to yourself.

At the very first sign that your long-buried feelings might make you violent toward yourself or anyone else, be sure to get help. At the very least, talk to a trusted, competent friend. If you have any doubt at all about the possibility of your own violence, do get professional help. This is an area where it is important to be safe, not sorry.

This is especially true for men who have been abused as boys. Childhood abuse, of any kind or combination—emotional, physical, or sexual—is typically tenacious in its ill effects and the therapeutic process of counseling can make a huge difference.

The same goes for men who may have feelings of rage for

their wives or partners and thus are tempted to domestic violence. They need to get involved in some kind of counseling process that will resolve their propensity quickly and peacefully. Men who are the victims of domestic violence have the same need. Although it is much more rare for men to be battered than for women, it definitely happens, and because it is atypical, it often causes shame and is frequently kept secret. The Three Steps to Emotional Fitness have been used successfully in domestic violence treatment programs.

Being involved in counseling is one of the fastest ways to grow and to overcome emotional challenges. Fortunately, the stigma that was once attached to counseling has lessened considerably. To believe that *I don't need anybody's help, I can do this myself* is, again, to believe the lies that have kept us half alive. It's stupid. Getting help when help is needed is smart. Getting help with a feeling that is challenging to you could be a very insightful expression of the third step.

It seems to do no good to dig up old feelings that have already been resolved, maybe long ago. These are different from buried feelings. They may have been buried before, but they have long since been identified and expressed and thus resolved, so let them be. At times, it is difficult to distinguish between buried feelings and just old feelings. Again, counseling will help.

A repetition seems worthwhile here: it can be harmful to bury pleasant, positive feelings such as feeling honored or complimented or excited or satisfied. These don't do the damage of their negative counterparts, but they do add to the population of repressed feelings in the burial vault. And especially, by burying these gems, the enjoyment of life is lessened and your personality is impoverished.

As you practice the three steps you will get better at them. Soon, they will become a natural part of your life, which is exactly what they are meant to be.

Talking with Children

How would you change the adult responses in the following dialogues to indicate that you accept the feeling, and still not let the kid get away with anything?

Boy: "Daddy, I'm tired."

Adult response: "You couldn't be tired, you just took a nap."

Boy: "I don't want to go to the baseball game."

Adult response: "What? What kind of kid doesn't like baseball?"

Boy: "It's cold in here."

Adult response: "No it's not. Take your jacket off."

Boy: "I'm mad at the coach. He's keeping me out of the game for being two minutes late for practice."

Adult response: "Well, it's your own fault, you shouldn't be late."

A Few Suggestions for Review

Nothing's Wrong is designed to be a brief treatment of how you can deal with your feelings in a healthy way. The disadvantage of being brief is the great amount of material that is not covered: the examples, techniques, and other related areas of life that have an effect on your feeling life. I encourage you to follow up your reading of this book with some of the books in the bibliography that follows.

In conclusion, here are a few ideas to review and keep in mind as you continue your adventure with feelings:

- Remember that you can achieve a healthy expression of your feelings. You are able to live a whole, integrated life that includes both thinking and feeling.

- Reading this book is an important accomplishment as well as a courageous step toward emotional fitness.

- Continue to talk about what's going on with you as a result of reading this book. Talk to friends and acquaintances and tell them how you feel. Ask for their input if you want it.

- You deserve to achieve what you want. You certainly deserve your birthright: an opportunity to live life fully, including the ability to express effectively the whole spectrum of your emotions.

- Other people in your life will benefit from your progress. It is probable that a spouse or partner will appreciate your courage to deal with this issue. Your children—especially sons—will certainly benefit. Wise, active fathering and mentoring, as expressions of the third step, will bear influence for generations to come.

- Don't be surprised if things get a little worse before they get a lot better, especially as you communicate more authentically with people. You may be making some significant changes, and people need time to notice, process their feelings, and respond. Persevere.

- Get help if you want it or need it. Don't hesitate. Often counseling does not have to last over a long period of time. Help might be in the form of a family counselor, other mental health professional, trained medical professional, or clergy trained in counseling (pastoral counselor). "Shop" for a counselor until you find one you like.

- Spend time with kids, yours or someone else's. There's no better way to observe and experience the spontaneity of feelings.

- Recall the power of your imagination and see what you are able to create in your life and in our world. Great men, like you, imagine greatly.

- Keep in mind: The more you are able to incorporate the Three Steps to Emotional Fitness into your life, the more you will become what you were always meant to be: both the adventurous and daring man on the moon, and the sensitive and lovable man in the moon.

I wish you success!

bibliography

Books

Bly, Robert. *The Sibling Society*. New York: Addison-Wesley
Publishing Co., 1996.

Bolman, Lee G. and Terrence E. Deal. *Leading with Soul: An
Uncommon Journey of Spirit*. San Francisco: Jossey-Bass,
1995.

Chittister, Joan. *Heart of Flesh: A Feminist Spirituality for
Women and Men*. New York: Eerdmans Publishing Co.,
1998.

Cornell, Joseph. *Listening to Nature*. Nevada City, Calif.: Dawn
Publications, 1987.

Faber, Adele and Elaine Mazlish. *How to Talk So Kids Will Listen
and Listen So Kids Will Talk*. New York: Avon Books, 1980.

Faludi, Susan. *Stiffed: The Betrayal of the American Man*. New
York: Harper Perennial, 2000.

Farrell, Warren. *Why Men Are the Way They Are*. New York:
Berkley Books, 1986.

Glennon, Will. *200 Ways to Raise a Boy's Emotional Intelligence*.
Berkeley: Conari Press, 2000.

Goleman, Daniel. *Destructive Emotions: How Can We Overcome Them? A Scientific Dialogue with the Dalai Lama.* New York: Bantam Doubleday Dell, 2003.

———. *Emotional Intelligence.* New York: Bantam Books, 1995.

———. *Working with Emotional Intelligence.* New York: Bantam Doubleday Dell, 2000.

Gurian, Michael. *The Good Son: Shaping the Moral Development of Our Boys and Young Men.* New York: Tarcher/Putnam, 1999.

Kindlon, Dan and Thompson, Michael. *Raising Cain: Protecting the Emotional Life of Boys.* New York: Ballantine Books, 1999.

Kundtz, David. *Stopping: How to Be Still When You Have to Keep Going.* Berkeley: Conari Press, 1998.

Kupers, Terry A. *Revisioning Men's Lives.* New York: The Guilford Press, 1993.

Levant, Ronald F. and William S. Pollack, eds. *A New Psychology of Men.* New York: Basic Books, 1995.

McKay, Matthew, Patrick Fanning, and Kim Paleg. *Couple Skills.* Oakland: New Harbinger Press, 1994.

Milam, James R. and Katherine Ketcham. *Under the Influence: A Guide to the Myths and Realities of Alcoholism.* New York: Bantam Books, 1984.

Oliver, Gary. *Real Men Have Feelings Too.* [Christian] Chicago: Moody Publishers, 1993.

Pollack, William. *Real Boys: Rescuing Our Sons from the Myths of Boyhood.* New York: Henry Holt, 1998.

Potter-Efron, Ron and Pat Potter-Efron. *Letting Go of Anger.* Oakland: New Harbinger Press, 1995.

Putnam, Robert. *Bowling Alone.* New York: Touchstone Books, 2001.

Real, Terrence. *I Don't Want to Talk about It.* New York: Fireside, Simon and Schuster, 1997.

Steiner, Claude. *When a Man Loves a Woman.* New York: Grove Press, 1986.

Tannen, Deborah. *You Just Don't Understand: Women and Men in Conversation.* New York: William Morrow & Co., Inc., 1991.

Viscott, David, M.D. *The Language of Feelings.* New York: Pocket Books, 1976.

Whyte, David. *The Heart Aroused: Poetry and the Preservation of the Soul in Corporate America.* New York: Currency, Doubleday, 1994.

———. *The House of Belonging.* Langley, Wash.: Many Rivers Press, 1997.

Web site

MenStuff: The National Men's Resource at *www.menstuff.org.* This is a site with many and varied resources for men.

permissions

Excerpt from "Captain Craig" by Edwin Arlington Robinson reprinted with permission from *Bartleby.com*

Epigraph from Ashleigh Brilliant copyright © Ashleigh Brilliant used by permission.

"Loaves and Fishes" from *The House of Belonging* by David Whyte. Copyright © 1997 by David Whyte. Reprinted by permission of the author and Many Rivers Press.

"Dear Abby" column as seen in *Dear Abby* by Abigail Van Buren a.k.a. Jeanne Phillips and founded by her mother Pauline Phillips. Copyright © Universal Press Syndicate. Reprinted with permission. All rights reserved.

"I go among the trees and sit still" from Wendell Berry's *Sabbaths*, used by permission. Copyright © Clearance Center.

about the author

David Kundtz holds graduate degrees in psychology and theology and a doctoral degree in pastoral psychology. Ordained in the 1960s, he worked as an editor and pastor until he left the ministry in 1982. He is currently a licensed family therapist and the director of Berkeley, California-based Inside Track Seminars, which specializes in stress management for the helping professions. He lives in Kensington, California and Vancouver, British Columbia.

Dr. Kundtz welcomes your communication and will make every effort to respond. He is especially interested in hearing from readers with feedback on the themes and practices of the book, and both he and Conari Press are genuinely interested in knowing your experiences. Let us hear from you.

Contact David Kundtz:

E-mail: *dk@stopping.com*

Mailing address: David Kundtz, c/o RedWheel/Weiser/ Conari Press, 368 Congress Street, Boston, MA 02210

Web site: *www.stopping.com*

Visit the Conari Web site: *www.conari.com*

Visit the Red Wheel/Weiser Web site: *www.redwheelweiser.com*

to our readers

Conari Press, an imprint of Red Wheel/Weiser, publishes books on topics ranging from spirituality, personal growth, and relationships to women's issues, parenting, and social issues. Our mission is to publish quality books that will make a difference in people's lives—how we feel about ourselves and how we relate to one another. We value integrity, compassion, and receptivity, both in the books we publish and in the way we do business.

Our readers are our most important resource, and we value your input, suggestions, and ideas about what you would like to see published. Please feel free to contact us, to request our latest book catalog, or to be added to our mailing list.

Conari Press
An imprint of Red Wheel/Weiser, LLC
P.O. Box 612
York Beach, ME 03910-0612
www.conari.com